Get Qualifications For What You Know and Can Do

A Personal Guide to APL

Susan Simosko

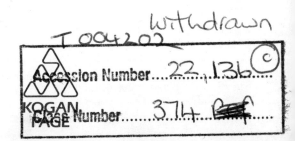

**To my sister, Nancy Rotolo
and my friends, Lillie Horton, Stephen Housely,
Sean McCarthy, and Elizabeth Shaw
in recognition of all they know and can do**

First published in 1992

Kogan Page Limited
120 Pentonville Road
London N1 9JN

© Susan Simosko, 1992

British Library Cataloguing in Publication Data

A CIP record for this book is available from the
British Library.

ISBN 0 7494 0475 2 Pbk
ISBN 0 7494 0724 7 Hbk

Typeset by DP Photosetting, Aylesbury, Bucks
Printed and bound in Great Britain by
Clays Ltd, St Ives plc

Contents

Foreword

In recent years a revolution has been taking place in training. At the centre of this revolution has been a growing awareness by business that the best way forward to ensure commercial success is to invest in an effective workforce and to maximize that investment by developing the skills and potential of every member of the organization's team.

This revolution would not have been possible without a new way of looking at the skills of individual people. Competence-based learning, which focuses on the needs of individuals, underpins the new and vitally important National Vocational Qualifications, an essential component of the skills revolution.

As a part of this revolution, many new opportunities are becoming available to allow and encourage individuals to take much greater control of their own learning and development. Accreditation of prior learning (APL), the subject of this interesting and timely book, provides one such important opportunity. APL will enable many people to participate in the emerging skills revolution and, at the same time, gain recognition and qualifications for their existing skills and knowledge.

In this way, APL is about personal growth. It, like this book, is important to all our futures.

TONY WEBB
Director of Education and Training
Confederation of British Industry

Preface

Not so many years ago, when I was still living and working in the United States, a woman telephoned me late one Friday afternoon. In a halting, almost cracking voice, she said, 'I have a very big problem. I wonder if you might help me.' I replied that I would be pleased to be of assistance if I could and asked her what her problem was. There was a long pause and then a deep breath. Finally the woman blurted out: 'Everyone, even my family, thinks I am stupid. I have raised a family, held both full- and part-time jobs, and contributed to a lot of community projects, but', she continued, 'I have no qualification of any sort and everyone else in my family does.' Then she gave a little laugh that only partially covered up her real feelings and said, 'It's really beginning to get to me . . . I suppose at my age it shouldn't be an issue, but it is. I want a qualification just like other people, one that will tell everyone that I'm as good as they are. I'm not really stupid, you know.'

I certainly had no doubts whatsoever about her intelligence! In so few words this woman had articulately summed up the hundreds of stories I hear each year about people who are held back in some aspect of their lives because they lack qualifications. For some people, like the woman above, the need for a qualification becomes an urgent matter of self-esteem. For others it means getting a better job; for still others it means getting a first job.

No matter what the reasons, in today's world obtaining a qualification that reflects what a person really knows and can do can be vitally important – both personally and professionally.

And for most adults, having to spend extended periods of time sitting in classrooms relearning what they already know – to say nothing of the hassle of getting to and from those classrooms – is an unnecessary stress at best and more likely, a terrible waste of their time, effort and potential. People today who want to develop themselves and earn qualifications need to do so in as flexible and personal a way as possible.

This book, then, provides an alternative route to help you obtain the qualifications you need or want. It is a practical book, one that you can use on your own or along with other materials provided by an educational or training organization. Its goal is to show you how you can make good use of all you already know and can do, so you, like my Friday afternoon caller who actually obtained a university degree, can get the qualifications you deserve. To that end, I hope you find it helpful.

ACKNOWLEDGEMENTS

For providing so much information about their APL policies and practices, I want to thank each of the lead bodies, awarding bodies, professional bodies and associations listed in Appendix 3.

A special thank you is also extended to the following organizations for allowing me to use or cite examples from their materials. These include: Bus and Coach Training Limited (BCT); Business and Technical Education Council (BTEC); City and Guilds of London Institute (C&G); Management Charter Initiative (MCI); RSA Examinations Board (RSA); Scottish Vocational Education Council (SCOTVEC); and Unit for the Development of Adult Continuing Education (UDACE).

I also want to extend a sincere thank you to Jonathan Stewart for his high-level professional support in the preparation of the manuscript and his attention to detail and to Gloria Savage for her helpful review of the manuscript and useful comments. Thank you too to Andrea Curry for her helpful illustrations.

Lastly, I want to thank my husband, Graham Debling, for his continued enthusiasm, encouragement, patience and very helpful suggestions.

Susan Simosko
Autumn 1991

Chapter 1

Give Yourself Credit

To get a qualification for what you *already* know and can do, you will need to ask yourself a lot of questions. For example, what kind of person are you? Are you someone who likes to:

- learn new things?
- take charge of your life?
- feel proud of what you accomplish?

If you answered 'yes' to even one of these questions, this book can help you learn many new things about yourself, take control of parts of your life you may have been ignoring and feel proud of what you have done. It can also help you build on your strengths, set new targets for yourself and show you how to reach them.

Most important of all, this book can help you receive recognition, credit and qualifications for what you already know and can do. It may be that you are hoping to receive promotion at work, or you are trying to find a new job, or you would just like to acquire a vocational or academic qualification to satisfy a long-standing dream. These are just some of the reasons why you may want to give yourself credit!

WHAT DOES 'GIVE YOURSELF CREDIT' REALLY MEAN?

Everyone likes to be recognized for what they do well. Even the shyest person is quietly pleased to be complimented. But so often in our busy lives many of us fail to receive the acknowledgement or praise we rightfully should enjoy. Not only do others fail to recognize our achievements, but sometimes we fail to recognize them in ourselves. It is not uncommon for some people who are really good at something to discount what they can do with throw-away comments such as 'Oh, anyone could do that,' or 'It's not such a big deal,' or 'I'm not an expert, just lucky!' All of us have met people who regularly talk themselves down. And yet think of all the things we and our friends and families have accomplished – in many cases without the benefit of any formal education or training: whether we are good in the kitchen, the garden, on the shop floor or in the board room, each of us has learned a lot by sorting out our lives, solving problems, working and living with others, trying new things, making the best use of the situations in which we find ourselves, and by making mistakes! It doesn't matter what our age, background or values are: all of us have learned a lot from our experiences.

So to credit yourself means first of all to recognize your own accomplishments, skills and abilities. Second, it involves getting further recognition by proving to someone else that you really know and can do what you claim. Each chapter of this book will help you to do both.

IS THERE A TERM TO DESCRIBE 'CREDIT YOURSELF'?

In Britain, the United States, Australia and many other nations, the idea of recognizing and crediting people's achievements is growing in use and popularity. The actual term that describes the process is 'Accreditation of Prior Learning' or 'APL' for short. (Sometimes you will hear other phrases such as 'assessment of prior experiential learning' or 'accreditation of prior achievements', which mean the same thing.)

Although the basic idea may be quite straightforward – that people should receive recognition and credit for what they know and can do – the phrase 'accreditation of prior learning' often needs some describing. 'Accreditation' means to recognize officially in some way. Generally we say that people receive accreditation towards formal qualifications. When they are accredited, they are recognized as having met the expectations of someone who is deserving of that qualification.

The difference between APL and more traditional routes to qualifications, however, is that people going though the APL process often do not have to take formal education or training courses in order to be accredited or receive credit towards a qualification. What they know and can do is considered equal to that of people completing formal programmes of study or training. And sometimes, of course, it is much more than just 'equal to'. APL allows individuals to receive formal recognition or credit towards a qualification because they can demonstrate in a variety of ways that they can meet the pre-defined standards of a course, training programme or a qualification.

The phrase 'prior learning' often raises another important question. Is there anything that a person knows and can do that has not been learned in the past? The answer is, of course not! 'Prior learning' in the context of APL means anything you have learned up to the point at which you are formally seeking recognition or credit. You may want to receive credit for things you do at work, or in your volunteer activities, or at home. You may also want to receive recognition or credit for courses or training programmes you took – or are taking – that did not lead to a formal qualification. The choice will be yours.

APL, then, is a process that allows you to seek credit or recognition – be accredited! – for what you know and can do, regardless of when, why or how you learned. It is a flexible process that allows you to present proof of your best self in order to receive the recognition, credit and qualifications you deserve.

WHERE DID APL COME FROM?

As an idea APL has been around for a long time. There is evidence to suggest that in various forms it was used in fifth-century China, in Europe during the Middle Ages with the Guild system and in the development of many of the world's great universities.

The basic principle that people often learn best by doing has also been part of the thinking of many great philosophers, inventors, artists and other famous people. Aristotle, Thomas Edison, Florence Nightingale, Duke Ellington, Vincent Van Gogh and Sir John Harvey Jones all provide good examples of people whose contributions to society have been without the benefit of the expected formal qualifications. All these people, and others like them, have shared a common belief that experience is often the best teacher.

Although the idea has been around for a long time, the actual process and the application to formal qualifications is relatively recent. APL developed in the USA during the 1970s. Originally called the assessment of prior learning, it started out as a large-scale research study that asked two critical questions:

1. Is it possible to equate non-college learning with the standards of traditional course work? and
2. Can people not in the educational system be assessed against those standards?

The answer to these important questions was an unequivocal 'yes'. Today, APL is offered at more than 1200 colleges and universities in the USA, often in cooperation with employers, unions, and trade associations.

WHY IS APL IMPORTANT IN BRITAIN?

We need only read the newspapers or listen to news reports to understand the very great importance of Britain's ability to compete in the world market. Few periods in history have put such pressure on nations to improve!

At issue is whether or not Britain will be able to maintain a competitive edge. Will its goods and services continue to have value in the world's marketplaces? Will its workforce be able to adapt to continued technological and social change? Will there be enough trained young people to fill all the jobs that will need to be filled in the future?

These questions may seem quite removed to many of us in our daily lives, but to government policy makers, employers, and other leaders of the nation, the answers will be critical to the future stability and quality of life for all of us. Only by keeping up the demand for quality goods and services; only by making sure the workforce can keep up with rapid change; and only by making sure that there are able people to fill all the necessary jobs will Britain be able to maintain its status as a world economic leader.

In this context, APL has an important role to play. It helps individuals to recognize their strengths and abilities. As a result, people often:

1. do not need to relearn what they already know and can do;
2. can obtain needed qualifications in less time and often while they are employed;
3. identify their own training and development needs and take control of their own progress;
4. demonstrate all they know and can do against national standards and qualifications; and
5. meet the needs of employers and others who want to ensure the quality and flexibility of their workforce.

As Britain, like many other countries, experiences a dramatic shift in the number of young people available to assume jobs in the next century, adults will be increasingly called on to fill new jobs and responsibilities. Some experts estimate that most of us will change jobs or careers six to ten times in the course of our lifetimes! And with each new job or responsibility we will be expected to learn and do new things. Retraining and often acquiring new qualifications will become a normal part of our lives. APL will help people receive recognition, credit, and qualifications for what they know and can do, thereby reducing retraining time, saving individuals and employers money, and encouraging people to take greater control of their own learning and development throughout their lives.

People who complete the APL process, regardless of the nation they live in, have said that the process makes them more aware of what they are good at, what their interests are, and how they like to learn. Britain, like most nations in the world, needs to have far greater numbers of people who know their strengths, have an interest in learning and are eager and self-confident enough to take up the challenge of life-long learning. APL may provide help!

APL AND YOU

While APL may be of help to the nation, first and foremost, you will want to think about how APL can help *you*. Each person beginning the APL process needs to have a clear idea of the potential benefits and expected outcomes of the process. Equally each person needs to know what the APL process involves. But let's begin with the potential benefits to *you*.

BENEFITS

At the outset it is important to say that APL is not always an easy or cheap option. It takes time, thought, perseverance and a certain amount of creative energy. And very seldom is it free. So although there are any number of options possible, APL also requires the payment of fees. But most people completing the process – those people who gain recognition, credit and/or qualifications – feel the time and money well worth it. APL can be an important way of investing in yourself and giving yourself a valuable bonus payment in the form of a national qualification.

As you begin to consider whether APL is for you, you may find the life stories of the six people described below helpful. Each person identified a real benefit that could be gained by going through the APL process. See if any of their reasons are similar to your own.

Case Studies
Clair M.

Clair is 38 years old and has been separated from her husband for three years. She has two children aged 13 and 15. She left school with an 'O' level but later returned to college to take up a commercial secretarial course. Unfortunately due to a family illness, she had to leave after completing only one term.

Her most recent full-time work was with a mid-sized company, working in the typing pool. Regrettably, the company ran into financial problems and closed down after Clair had been with them just 18 months. She had been hoping to get out of the pool and secure a personal secretary post.

Since that job came to an end, Clair has been working for a temporary agency and has been out on a number of different assignments. She is particularly pleased that one firm keeps asking for her personally. She thinks she would like to work for them full-time but they require all staff to have qualifications.

Over the years, Clair has learned a lot – not just from her paid employment but from those things she does in the community and with her children. Some of the specific things she knows and can do include: preparing and writing routine letters and memos; operating a computer for purposes of basic word processing; answering and directing phone calls; setting up filing systems; administering first aid; playing the piano; and organizing herself and other people.

Clair decided to seek APL in order to get a qualification to improve her chances of getting a better job. As a single parent, it is not easy for her to make ends meet (even with the support provided by her husband). In addition, she is tired of always being on the first rung of the career ladder and feels she must do more with her life, especially as her children will soon be making lives of their own. Clair hopes that through APL she will be able to make good use of the skills and abilities she already has in order to get the qualifications she needs more quickly.

Erik S.

Erik is 28 and single. He came to Britain to study and two years ago became engaged to Margaret. Although he began a degree programme, he dropped out – mostly because he was, as he puts it now, 'a little bit bored and definitely immature'.

Before coming to Britain, Erik had travelled extensively with his family and had earned a number of certificates in his home country, all of which had enabled him to enter a British university with ease. His family had high expectations of him and were very disappointed when he decided to drop out.

A businessman friend of the family who resides in Britain offered to give Erik a job on a temporary basis until he either went back to university or returned to his homeland. But within no time, Erik had carved out a permanent position with the firm in the area of computer technology. Erik thoroughly enjoyed the work and regularly came up with creative solutions to problems which even surprised some of the more senior people in the firm. He is well liked throughout the firm and the owner of the company, his parents' friend, now wants to help Erik develop so he will have even more opportunities within the company.

Erik finds work challenging and interesting – unlike his initial university experience. But he also recognizes now that there is a lot more to learn and do. He would like to have a qualification – the degree he once aspired to – if just to prove that he is as good as anybody else. He also believes that with time, the degree might qualify him for a good job in his native country, should he wish to return once he and Margaret are married.

Erik and his employer both believe that APL will enable Erik to reach his educational and professional goals. Further, the employer believes that investing in Erik's development will ultimately help the organization by improving the quality and diversity of Erik's contribution. He is willing to take the risk that Erik might leave after completing his degree programme.

Sally B.

Sally is 55 years old. She has been married 35 years and is proud of her three children and four grandchildren. Until recently, Sally has been active in a number of local activities. At one time or another she has done voluntary work in the local prison and the local hospital and, most important, she has been responsible for coordinating the largest charity in her town. Over the years, the charity has raised thousands of pounds and most people attribute the level of success to Sally's continued ability to organize and motivate other people.

Five years ago, Sally began to suffer seriously from arthritis. Now she is often in so much pain that she has had to reduce her activities considerably. She can no longer do voluntary work and last year she had to give up the charity she so enjoyed. She often feels depressed and, as she puts it, 'useless'.

A friend told Sally about APL – not because she felt Sally would necessarily want a qualification – but because she felt that working towards a new goal in her own time might help Sally recognize all the strengths and abilities she still had and give her a new perspective on what she might do next with her life. Sally decided, with the support of her family, to find out what it was all about before making a firm commitment.

Brian A.

Brian is in his early forties, divorced and a professional engineer. He completed his qualifications early in life and struggled on for more than ten years with a marriage that wasn't working for him or his wife. Although it was sad at the time, when the divorce finally came through, Brian was mostly relieved.

During the stormy years of his marriage, Brian had increasingly thrown himself into work. Apart from his much loved dog, Brian seemed to have little time for anything other than work. He was in before everyone else and left long after everyone had gone. Since his divorce, he has dated a little but finds he has no interest in becoming a social butterfly.

Because of his hard work, Brian has received frequent pay rises and promotions. He now finds himself in charge of a team of engineers as well as technical and support staff. People within the organization view him as a manager; he views himself as a hard-working engineer trying to get on with the job.

Increasingly, however, he is having problems with a number of people in his team. There is a lot of internal bickering, people openly question the work priorities he sets and support staff have sent him a stream of memos questioning recent pay awards which were lower than in previous years. He often feels 'in over his head' as he describes it and wonders what he could be doing differently. He doesn't seem to have trouble managing budgets or other company resources, just the people!

Most recently Brian and his boss have discussed the possibility of Brian taking some management development courses, especially in the area of managing people. Brian's boss has also told him about the APL service being offered at the local college and has asked him to go through the process so that the company might see whether or not it could be helpful to others within the organization. Brian doesn't really know anything about APL but he is eager to reduce the tension he feels at the bottom of his stomach every time a new personnel problem lands on his desk. He's happy to go along with the boss's request.

Gita W.

When Gita was very young her family emigrated to Britain. Although she completed school, the main focus of Gita's life was the clothing shop her parents struggled to keep open. Gita and her younger brothers and sisters all helped out doing everything from sweeping the floor to stocking shelves and one way or another the shop managed to grow.

As the oldest child, Gita had been the one who learned English first. Her parents, while they spoke a little, were far more comfortable speaking in their native language. As a result, Gita often found herself making phone calls to importers, accountants, insurance brokers and so forth when she was still a young teenager. By the time she was 19, she did most of the day-to-day management of the shop, although her parents still made all the important decisions.

As Gita developed an active social life in the local community, she and her parents began to fall out. It was a very painful time for everyone and in the end, Gita left her family home and the shop.

For several years, Gita worked at odd jobs, always wishing there was a way she could turn back the clock and work with her parents again. But she knew this wasn't to be.

In her late twenties Gita met Ann. The two women thought if they could pool their very limited resources and combined energies, they would be able to open their own clothing shop. They worked out all the details on paper and went to the local bank manager for a start-up loan. Although the bank manager said their plan looked 'interesting', the loan was never approved. Gita and Ann both were back to doing jobs well below their ability.

Gita heard about APL and immediately sensed that it could be of value to her. She felt she urgently needed proof of all she knew and could do and that a recognized national qualification could be the answer to some of her problems.

Bill W.

Bill is in his early forties, married, with one child, 19 years old. He has no previous qualifications.

For the past nine years he has been working in a small car-maintenance garage. He routinely carries out repairs on a wide range of vehicles. Before joining this garage, he worked for a local tyre and battery company which, regrettably for Bill, closed shortly after a national company moved in near by.

His current employer is getting on in years and increasingly does not seem as interested in the business as he once was. This has had a serious effect on trade, with the garage failing to attract new customers. Existing customers think highly of Bill's work but he fears for his long-term job security and wants to do something about it. He would also like to earn a higher salary and in truth thinks he can handle more responsibility, especially since the owner generally leaves Bill in charge when he is away.

He has applied for a number of other jobs, but has not even been invited for an interview. Most of the companies in which he is interested seem to want either qualifications or more extensive formal training than Bill has had.

Some of the things Bill knows and can do include: carrying out routine service and safety checks, using a wide range of tools; inspecting tyres and wheels and ensuring that they meet the legal requirements and using a wide range of equipment to replace and repair tyres; diagnosing and repairing faults in transmission, ignition and exhaust systems; maintaining stock supplies; operating and balancing the till; and coaching the local swimming team. Indeed Bill thinks that the success of the swimming team may be one of the

Checklist 1.1   *Is APL for you?*

I think APL could help me because I:

___ need to find a job

___ need a qualification

___ would like promotion

___ would like a qualification

___ want to change directions

___ want to find a better job

___ want to prove myself in a new way

___ want to develop myself

___ want to gain access to a particular course or training programme

___ want to complete a qualification I started earlier in my life

___ (write out any extra or different reasons of your own) _____

_____

_____

_____

---

main reasons he gets on so well with the younger men in the garage (many of whom have qualifications) and the customers, and why the owner leaves him in charge so regularly.

Bill views APL as an opportunity to earn credit and, he hopes, qualifications that will enable him to get a better job but he also believes that he has a lot to learn as well. Since he has only really worked for two companies, he wants to learn what else he *should* know and be able to do to build on the skills he already has.

IS APL FOR YOU?

As these six stories illustrate, people decide to seek APL for a wide variety of reasons. For every one of these stories, there are dozens more. To help you decide whether APL could be useful to you, you will want to look at all the possible benefits and write them down. Checklist 1.1 may help to get you started. Put a tick next to all the statements that seem to apply to you and your situation.

No matter what your reasons, APL could be a valuable way forward for you. Like all other training or education programmes, however, APL cannot provide you with a guarantee. It is only a tool that will allow you to consider new options for yourself, help you build on your strengths, take greater responsibility for your own learning and development and add to your self-confidence and sense of accomplishment. The remaining chapters of this book tell you how the system works and what you will have to do to get the recognition, credit and qualifications you deserve.

Chapter 2

What's It All About?

Great changes are under way in Britain – changes that are beginning to recognize the strengths and needs of each individual wanting or needing qualifications. To no small extent, the entire education and training system is undergoing a revolution, a 'quiet' one that will provide greater opportunity for people of all ages and backgrounds to learn, develop and be recognized for their achievements.

APL is one of the important outcomes of this quiet revolution. So it is important for you to develop a clear picture of what APL actually is and what you will be expected to do to receive the credit and qualifications you want.

THE APL PROCESS

Thus far we have talked about the *idea* of APL and its potential benefits. But before you can really decide whether or not APL is for you, you will need to know exactly what the APL process is.

APL involves six distinct steps. At each one, you will need to undertake certain activities and make various decisions. There also will be specific outcomes or results that you can expect. It is important to add, too, that during the APL process, there will be a number of other people to help you. It is useful to know the roles of each of these people and what you can expect from them.

But first, let's take a look at each APL step, the activities you will be doing, the decisions you will be making and the outcomes you can expect.

The six steps of APL include:

1. Identifying your strengths.
2. Selecting a qualification, course or training programme for which you want recognition or credit.

3. Matching your strengths with the requirements of the qualification, course or training programme you have selected.
4. Gathering and preparing the proof that you really know and can do what you say you can.
5. Being assessed by a recognized 'assessor'.
6. Being accredited (ie getting a qualification or a certificate which rewards what you have achieved).

We'll take a brief look at each step now and then take a much closer look in later chapters.

Step 1: Identifying your strengths
During this step you will need to take a careful look at all you know and can do and begin to focus on those things for which you want credit and recognition. This may sound like a pretty simple process – and for some people it is – but to do a really good job can require time and thought.

Activities: Some of the activities of this first step include:

- reviewing your past experiences;
- identifying your accomplishments;
- describing your day-to-day responsibilities;
- talking with others familiar with what you know and can do; and
- writing down what you are really good at.

Decisions: What you include in these activities is totally up to you. You will need to make decisions about yourself and what has been and *is* important to you. The work sheets in Chapter 4 will help you begin this process in a straightforward way.

Expected outcome: At the end of this first step, you should have a good picture of yourself. Indeed, you may be surprised at all the things you know and can do! This picture of yourself is often called a 'personal profile'.

Step 2: Selecting a qualification, course or training programme for which you want recognition or credit

Activities: Your activities at this step will depend very much on how clear you are about why you are seeking credit or recognition for what you know and can do. If you are unclear, or have doubts about what you should be – or might be – seeking through APL, some of your activities will be to:

- obtain information;
- talk to others; and
- ask questions.

Even if you are quite clear about your objectives in seeking APL, you will still need to:

- contact the organization or institution offering the qualification, course or training programme in which you are interested;
- confirm that what you are hoping to achieve is consistent with the programme or service of the centre you have contacted; and
- collect all the relevant information that will allow you to begin.

Decisions: Deciding what qualification, course or training programme to seek credit and recognition for is one of the biggest decisions you will need to make as part of your APL work. Many people who are interested in APL – at least in the idea – often have difficulty deciding exactly what to aim for. The next chapter will provide you with some of the information you will need in order to make your decision. Most organizations offering an APL service also will be prepared to offer you help and guidance to make this and other important decisions. Usually an APL centre will appoint a trained 'adviser' to work with you through this and all other stages of the APL process.

Expected outcomes: The main outcome of this step in the APL process is a clear target. Whether you decide to obtain a certificate, a diploma, degree or some other form of qualification or recognition, once you have made your decision, you will be able to develop a clear plan of action.

Step 3: Matching your strengths with the requirements of the qualification, course or training programme you have selected

Activities: This step will involve you in four main activities:

- obtaining and reading the requirements or standards of the qualification, course or training programme you have selected;
- completing a checklist or other type of form to begin to match what you know and can do with what is expected;
- identifying ways you might be able to prove that you really know and can do what you are claiming; and
- identifying any gaps between what you know and can do and what is expected of you.

Decisions: You will be making at least three major decisions at this step:

- you will need to decide whether or not there is a close enough match between what you know and can do and the requirements or standards of the qualification, course or training programme to allow you to gain the credit or recognition you would like;
- you will need to decide on the type and availability of the proof you will need to bring forward; and

- if you have decided that you know and can do *most*, if not all, of what is expected, you will need to decide how you can fully meet the requirements by learning or developing further.

Expected outcome: Really there will be two outcomes from this step: first you will have a clear plan for identifying the way in which you will prove what you know and can do, and second, you will have a plan for undertaking new learning or development so you can meet *all* the requirements you will be expected to meet.

Step 4: Gathering and preparing the proof that you really know and can do what you say you can

Activities: At this step you will be into the heart of your APL work. The major activities will include:

- gathering or producing examples of your work or other 'evidence' that can serve as proof of what you know and can do;
- getting other people to write letters on your behalf;
- putting all these materials into a file or folder called a 'portfolio';
- completing a range of forms that your centre will give you; and
- sometimes writing a brief description or 'personal report' which will show how the material or 'evidence' in your 'portfolio' relates to the expectations of the qualification, course or training programme you have selected.

Decisions: You will be making many decisions at this important step in your APL work, all of which will be directed at helping you prove in the best ways you can that you really know and can do the things you say you can. Some of the decisions you will be making include:

- deciding exactly what to include in your portfolio;
- deciding who could best write on your behalf; and
- deciding what to include in your personal report.

Expected outcome: The main outcome of this step of the work will be a well-organized, easy-to-read portfolio which fully reflects all you know and can do. Your portfolio will be the proof that will take you to the next step in the APL process.

Step 5: Being assessed by a recognized 'assessor'

Activities: Once you have completed your portfolio it will be reviewed and evaluated by a trained specialist called an assessor. The job of the assessor is to make sure that you really do know and can do what you claim. Your portfolio is the starting point of that confirmation. However, often the assessor may want to meet you to ask you questions about the material in your portfolio or about what you know and can do. For this reason there are a range of other activities you might have to complete during this step. These could include:

- answering questions about the evidence in your portfolio;
- describing in more detail what you know and can do;
- demonstrating some aspect of your work; and
- gathering or producing more evidence.

Decisions: Many of the decisions made at this point in the process will not be yours. They will be those of the assessor(s) who will decide whether or not you are entitled to receive the credit or recognition you are seeking.

Expected outcomes: The most obvious and satisfying outcome of this phase of your APL work will be that your assessor will recommend that you receive the recognition, credit or qualification you are seeking. Sometimes, however, people seeking credit through APL need to do additional work in a particular area. In these cases, the outcome may be that you do not receive the credit or recognition *yet*. Rather, you will have an opportunity to improve in one or more ways, as suggested by your assessor, before trying again.

Step 6: Being accredited

Activities: At this step, you will have nothing to do! Assuming you have been recommended for accreditation, all your hard work is done. The responsibility lies with someone else to award you the credit or recognition you are seeking. Just who this is depends on the type of qualification or credit you identified originally. Some of the possibilities are identified in Chapter 3.

Decisions: The decisions made at this point are between the organization awarding you the credit and your assessor. The awarding organization, sometimes called an awarding body, will want to make sure that the assessor conducted your assessment properly and fairly. A representative of the organization may visit your centre and actually look at portions of your portfolio with your assessor. Only after he or she is satisfied that you have been assessed correctly and that the evidence you presented really reflected the expectations of the qualification, will you receive the credit or qualifications you were seeking.

Expected outcomes: The primary outcome of this step is that you receive the credit or qualification you set out to obtain.

All this may seem like a lot to do! And indeed there is a lot to do. But remember almost always your APL work can be done in your own time and at home or in your office or wherever you feel most comfortable. Remember APL is *not* a course or training programme. It is a process that lets you:

- identify your own strengths and build on them constructively;
- select your own outcome – the qualification, course or training programme of your choice;
- influence how you are assessed; and
- develop your own plan of action.

And of course, APL can save you valuable time, energy and sometimes money. With APL, you take responsibility for your own actions and decisions. No one is looking over your shoulder telling you what you have to do; most of the people you will meet during your APL work will be there to help you.

At some point, probably early on in the process, you will want to locate an APL centre. This could be a college of further education, a polytechnic, a private training provider or even your employer.

You may want to begin the APL process on your own, using the guidelines in this book, or wait until you locate a nearby centre. Either way the decision will be yours. Remember, with APL you will have a lot of choices. So be prepared!

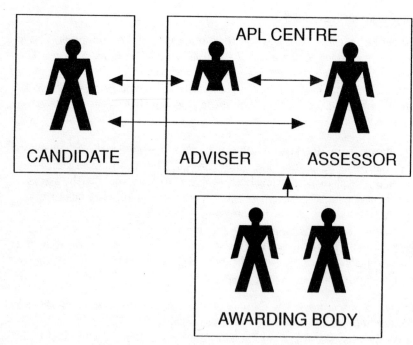

Figure 2.1   *Key players in the APL process*

Remember too that most centres offering APL services provide people – APL candidates, as they are usually called – with lots of help and support. So although you are responsible for doing your own APL work, you don't have to feel isolated. Just because you will be responsible, it doesn't mean you have to suffer! Figure 2.1 provides you with a visual description of most of the key players in the APL process.

Case Study

This is how one person, David, went through these six steps. He read this book and began to identify the things he was really good at. He also talked through with his family and friends the new direction he was hoping to take in his work and the qualification he needed to make that transition. Next he contacted several colleges of further education in his area to see what was available at each. He asked for information about the range of qualifications on offer and about the opportunities for APL.

He then enrolled with the college that seemed best suited to his needs and attended a workshop for adults returning to college who were interested in APL. There he had an opportunity to match his strengths with the expectations of the qualification he wanted. He also had a chance to meet and talk with others, like himself, who were also trying to change their lives in some significant way. Later he met an APL adviser too, who helped him to think about the ways he could prove what he already knew and could do.

When it came to gathering and preparing the proof he needed, David collected together several examples of his work and also requested and received detailed letters about his accomplishments from his previous and current employers.

He put all these materials into a folder, called a portfolio, and prepared a brief personal report which described some of the 'missing links' in his proof.

Once his portfolio had been accepted, he met an assessor. During this meeting he was asked a number of questions about his work. Most of the questions related to areas in which David had very little or no concrete evidence.

After his assessor told him he had been successful in meeting all the requirements, he waited impatiently for the qualification itself to arrive. When it did, he and his family celebrated and David planned his next steps to seek a new job.

Chapter 3
Using The System

With good reason, you may indeed wonder exactly what *the* system is. The simple answer is: it is the complex world of education, training and qualifications. As you will have realized from reading about the APL process, knowing something about the system will help you make good decisions at different steps. This chapter will provide you with some of the basic information that will help you to:

- ask the right questions;
- get the information you need; and
- get the most you can out of the system.

If it has been some time since you were in school, college or university the current world of education, training and qualifications will probably seem very different from the one you will remember. But if you are determined to receive the recognition, credit and qualifications you want and deserve, you will soon find yourself an expert in using the system to good effect. Learning to use the system may be a bit like peeling off the tough outer skin of a piece of fruit: once you finish the job, you are in store for a treat. Let's begin by answering a few key questions.

WHERE IS APL OFFERED?

Most often APL is available at colleges of further and higher education, polytechnics and universities. Some employers, professional bodies and private training organizations also offer APL. It is important to add, however, that APL is still a relatively new idea. It is not universally available at all education and training organizations. You may need to be a bit of a detective to find the centre nearest to you. Your local Training and Enterprise Council (TEC) should be able to help you and often local libraries can help in your search too. You can also write to the organizations listed in Appendix 3 to learn more about the availability of APL in your area.

HOW SHALL I KNOW WHICH QUALIFICATION TO CHOOSE?

This is a hard question because so many changes are under way in the education and training system. This chapter will describe systematically the various types of qualifications there are, let you know where they are available, and help you identify the important questions you may still want to ask.

It will not be necessary for you to memorize all the information that follows: it is provided only as a tool so that you will be well prepared to begin the APL process. You can always refer back to it when you need to.

TRADITIONAL ROUTES TO QUALIFICATIONS

Traditionally people have received qualifications at the end of a course or training programme. These qualifications provide an indication of what they learned during a specified period of study. Holding a particular qualification is often important to get on another course too. Schools, colleges, universities and professional bodies all issue various types of qualifications. You may be familiar with one or more of the following.

SCHOOL QUALIFICATIONS

Some examples of school qualifications include:

- General Certificate of Education (GCE) 'O' and 'A' Levels
- Scottish General Certificate of Education (SGCE) 'O' and 'H' Grades
- Certificate of Secondary Education (CSE)
- General Certificate of Secondary Education (GCSE)

To receive any of these qualifications, students were and are expected to take and pass examinations.

HIGHER EDUCATION

Following the successful completion of the 'O', 'A', or 'H' grade entrance requirements, a person would be eligible to go on to higher education in a polytechnic or university to study for a diploma or degree. This might be in any range of subject areas from biology to English literature, to history, to theoretical mathematics, to music and so forth.

FURTHER EDUCATION

Alternatively, a person could complete school with GCSEs and enrol in a college of further education, often for a period of one to two years. Frequently this course of study would be vocationally orientated, that is, the person would learn a particular set of skills, knowledge and understanding related to employment, eg, hairdressing, engineering, catering, business studies and so forth. If the individual were successful in passing the examinations at the end of this period of study, he or she would receive a 'vocational' qualification.

Unlike the degree which is awarded by the polytechnic or university the student has attended, vocational qualifications earned at the colleges of further education are awarded by a range of national organizations called awarding bodies. You may have heard of some of the larger ones such as:

- City and Guilds of London Institute (C&G);
- Business and Technical Education Council (BTEC);[1]
- Royal Society of Arts (RSA); and
- Scottish Vocational Education Council (SCOTVEC).[2]

There are many others, some of which are listed in Appendix 3. Although there are significant differences among these organizations, in general they are responsible for ensuring that the programmes of study offered by colleges of further education are sound and that the testing or assessment of students is carried out in a consistent and fair way. Some, like C&G and RSA actually provide and grade examinations for students.

As a group, these awarding bodies are responsible in one way or another for monitoring the standards and practices within further education. As you saw in step six of the APL process, they play a major role in monitoring good practice in APL.

---

[1] BTEC was formed by the combination of the Business Education Council (BEC) and the Technician Education Council (TEC).
[2] SCOTVEC was formed similarly by combining the Scottish Business Education Council (SCOTBEC) and the Scottish Technician Education Council (SCOTEC)

PROFESSIONAL QUALIFICATIONS

A third group of qualifications are awarded by organizations such as professional bodies and trade associations, training boards, etc. These usually relate to a particular occupation. Sometimes it is not possible to work in the occupation if you don't have the qualification. For example chartered accountants, doctors and chartered engineers have to be qualified. Sometimes, for example in association with apprenticeship programmes, training board certificates (eg the Agricultural Skills Tests) were – or are – taken with a qualification awarded by one of the national awarding bodies such as C&G.

ALTERNATIVE ROUTES

Traditional vocational qualifications are not always gained by going to college full time. Some people may have entered apprenticeship programmes after school in which they worked and went to college on a 'day-release' basis; others may have participated in a Youth Training Scheme (YTS) and again, attended college on a part-time basis. Some professional qualifications are taken by correspondence courses and increasingly alternative types of instruction – not just sitting in the classroom – are helping people to complete a wide range of education and training programmes. These types of instruction include television courses or other 'open' or 'distance' learning courses.

These routes to vocational qualifications are still widely available and in demand, but increasingly a whole new set of qualifications is changing the face of the British qualification system. These new qualifications are called National Vocational Qualifications (NVQs) in England, Wales and Northern Ireland, and Scottish Vocational Qualifications (SVQs) in Scotland.

WHAT ARE NVQs AND SVQs?

NVQs and SVQs are based on a different idea from most traditional qualifications. Unlike traditional qualifications which are awarded only at the end of a programme of study, these new qualifications are based on the idea of 'competence', which is a word we hear used in many different ways all the time. But in the context of qualifications, the word competence has a very precise meaning. It means:

the ability to perform activities to the standards generally expected in the work place.

In other words, the new qualifications relate directly to what people *know and can do* – not just to what they study.

Like traditional qualifications, NVQs and SVQs relate to specific occupational areas such as agriculture, catering, health and beauty therapy, etc. But unlike most traditional qualifications, these qualifications have a very different structure. Whereas traditional qualifications are awarded after one or two years of study, NVQs and SVQs are awarded when people have demonstrated that they can do what is expected – without reference to any particular period of time.

Although it is possible – often necessary, in fact – to study in a college or training centre to earn one of these qualifications, since they are based on what people actually do, many people will be able to acquire NVQs and SVQs in the normal course of their work. Some people – like you perhaps – will be able to obtain part or all of an NVQ or SVQ through APL. Still others may attend college part time and complete the requirements of the qualification in work.

What makes all this possible is the way in which these new qualifications are described. Each of the new qualifications spells out in detail what is expected of the person hoping to achieve it.

Both NVQs and SVQs are based on something called Units of Competence, which describe these expectations or 'standards', as they are most often called. A unit represents a particular area of competence that is regarded as important in the workplace. For example, in management some unit titles include:

- Contribute to the recruitment and selection of personnel.
- Create, maintain and enhance effective working relationships.
- Exchange information to solve problems and make decisions.

Groups of units put together form the basis of the new qualifications, but you can get credit for as little as a single unit if you can demonstrate that you are competent in that area.

A unit is not necessarily an area of *study*; nor is it linked to a set period of time. It is a statement of what a competent individual should know and be able to do in the workplace. As you will see in Chapter 5, the way in which these units are structured and described makes them particularly useful to people who are already competent and want to prove it – in other words, people who want to receive credit, recognition and qualifications for what they already know and can do. Colleges and training organizations may organize their curriculum around units, but it is only when people can demonstrate that they are fully competent that they can be accredited.

As shown in Figure 3.1, the National Council for Vocational Qualifications (NCVQ) monitors these new qualifications and makes sure they meet the needs of the people for whom they are intended. NCVQ itself *does not* award qualifications. It works with a range of different awarding bodies in the monitoring process.[3]

In conjunction with these new qualifications, there have been many other changes taking place. To see just how many, it is useful to compare briefly the traditional system with the one which is just emerging.

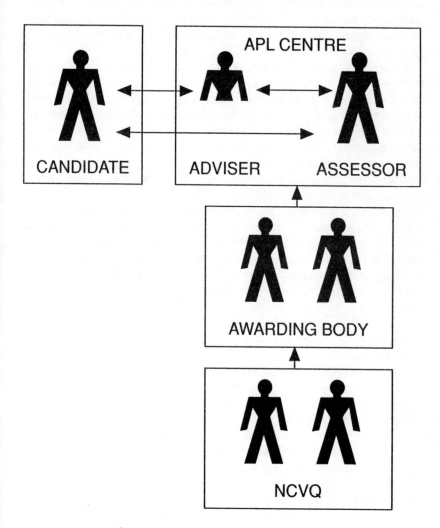

Figure 3.1 *NVQ Monitoring Process*

[3] For the interested reader, Appendix 1 provides a brief description of how and why these new qualifications were developed.

THE TRADITIONAL SYSTEM

In the traditional system, students were most often expected to learn as much as they could from what the teacher taught. Whether the students were in school, college, university or even in work, they were supposed to learn and prove that they had learned what the teacher taught. Sometimes the teachers lectured; sometimes they gave assignments or asked students to write papers. Generally students were said to pass the course only when they passed formal examinations.

Under the traditional system, it was assumed that the best learning occurred in schools, colleges or universities and that if students did everything they were expected to do within a specified time, they would be successful. Not much attention or value was given to all those things people learned outside the classroom. (It is perhaps worth remembering the story of Albert Einstein who nearly failed in school more than once. His theory of relativity which revolutionized modern science was not the outgrowth of a classroom lecture or assignment, but rather the result of Einstein's own curiosity and personal investigation.)

In addition, students were expected to be passive. It was not anticipated that they would be able to contribute in any meaningful way to what the teacher was presenting. They were expected to trust the judgements and decisions of their teachers – generally without question – and in tests provide the right answer to the questions the teacher posed.

In more traditional education and training organizations many educators and trainers also believed that to make sure a test or assessment was fair, the learners or students should not know what was to be in the test. And of course, it was assumed that pain and anxiety were a necessary part of all good assessment!

How many of us grew up in educational situations that were built on these beliefs and myths? Is it any wonder that many people found formal education less than appealing and helpful? The traditional system seemed designed more to exclude people from education and training, rather than to encourage them to use it to their best advantage.

In fairness, of course, many people found some of their teachers helpful – maybe even inspirational – and felt they were treated fairly throughout their educational experience. Many people also thrived in the traditional system and were able to meet their own personal goals.

Many more people, however, have felt excluded from formal education and training, viewing it as something for the other guy, the one who is already well along the educational qualification path. The new world of education and training is changing all of that.

THE EMERGING SYSTEM

The emerging system is being built on the idea that anyone who wants or needs a qualification should have an opportunity to obtain it. NVQs and SVQs have been or are being developed to cover a full range of occupational areas, many of which never before had any qualifications. These qualifications are designed to indicate that the person who holds one is *occupationally* competent, not just that he or she has completed a particular course of study. It is intended that the new qualifications will cover occupations from the shop floor to the board room. Appendix 2 provides a list of many of the occupational areas to be covered in the new system of qualifications.

There are many other changes under way in the education and training system. Many of these will be of great use to you in your APL work. Let's take a look at some of the more major ones.

- Most education and training organizations are focusing much more on the needs of *individuals*. They are providing advisers and mentors to help each person meet his or her goals.
- They are recognizing that what people know and can do is often learned through work, voluntary activities or in the home – not just in the classroom.
- Programmes of study are being broken down into smaller segments so that people have more *flexibility* in the way they learn and when.
- Assessment is being viewed as a natural part of learning and development, not just a cause for pain and suffering at the end of a course.
- Many employers are offering opportunities for their employees to gain NVQS or SVQs and many are working cooperatively with particular awarding bodies.
- Special programmes are being set up to help people who have been away from formal education and training to re-enter the system, often on their own terms and with a lot of support.
- Because of the shift in population to fewer numbers of school leavers, some colleges, polytechnics and universities are actively *recruiting more adults.*
- There are new opportunities for people to progress at their own rate within and across academic and vocational programmes.

Depending on what you need and want out of the education and training system, you will want to make use of as many of these new opportunities as possible.

A TRANSITION PERIOD

In Chapter 2 we said that Britain was undergoing a 'quiet revolution'. Indeed the scope and level of change is very significant. But it is important to recognize that as you begin your APL work, 'the revolution' is far from over. Indeed throughout the nation the traditional system and the new system often run head on into one another, even within the same college, polytechnic, university, awarding body or employer-based training programme. So be prepared!

As you begin your investigation to find an appropriate APL centre, a qualification and maybe a programme for new learning, you may find yourself caught up in some of the powerful tensions that have arisen in the midst of all the change. No doubt you will need to:

- be persistent;
- ask questions;
- say what you want and need; and
- be prepared to negotiate.

On the other hand, as we shall see in the next few chapters, you have every right to expect to have your questions answered, to receive help and support to achieve what you want and need, and to participate fully in the decisions made about or for you. Increasingly people in education and training are coming to realize that individuals, regardless of their age or background, learn best and achieve the most when they:

- enjoy what they are doing;
- know what is expected of them; and
- have control over how they learn and accomplish.

Many of the programmes and services being implemented across the country are now being geared to promoting these opportunities. APL provides a first-rate example.

WHAT NOW?

The education and training system may seem confusing, even maze-like. Even so, it is better to be prepared by knowing something about it than to be surprised when you begin contacting some of the APL centres in your area. As we move to looking in detail at the APL process and what you will want to do, you may want to refer to the information in this chapter from time to time. You may also want to make a list of questions you already have about the new or, for that matter, the traditional, education and training system. It might be worthwhile to jot them down now to make sure you don't forget what else you want or need to know.

Checklist 3.1 *Questions I have about the education and training system*

1. ————————————————————————————

————————————————————————————

2. ————————————————————————————

————————————————————————————

3. ————————————————————————————

————————————————————————————

4. ————————————————————————————

————————————————————————————

5. ————————————————————————————

————————————————————————————

Chapter 4

Getting Started

Now that you have an overview of APL and an idea of the system in which it is operating, you are ready to begin the process. In this chapter you will identify your strengths and what you want to receive credit for, and take a look at some of the help and support you can expect from the APL centre you choose. But let's begin with you and what you know and can do!

IDENTIFYING YOUR STRENGTHS

As described in Chapter 2, identifying your strengths is the first step in the APL process. Some people are pretty clear about what they are good at and other people really aren't too sure. Either way, there is always something new to learn about ourselves, so it is worth taking a closer look.

But as you begin this process you may be saying, 'Well I know what I'm good at but I can't/don't want/am unable to get qualifications for *that*.' If you are having thoughts like this, it is worth reassuring you now: just because you are good at something doesn't mean you either want or need a qualification to prove it. You may be good at a whole range of things, only one of which you want to receive recognition and qualifications for, even though it's not the 'main' thing you do. Consider the example of Helen.

Case Study

For more than ten years Helen had been employed as a personal secretary. She had worked for the managing director and had been given the opportunity to develop herself in any number of ways – by taking courses, by supervising a number of part-time staff and by taking on added responsibility on a regular basis.

But when Helen decided to get started with APL the one thing she was very sure of was that she didn't want a qualification in a secretarial subject. Although her job was 'OK' as she put it, she really wanted to become a qualified baker and change careers entirely. For as many years as she could remember, she had loved baking and had taken a number of courses at the local college, had read books, and, most important, had developed a small catering business from her home that specialized in fancy cakes. That is the area in which she wanted recognition and a qualification. Although she was proud of her work as a secretary, she felt she could be doing more creative and challenging work and wanted to make a fresh start in something new. However, she wasn't sure which catering qualification she wanted.

Lots of people are like Helen. You may be one of them. For this reason it is important to look at all the things you are good at and see how they relate to what you want to do next in your life.

Sometimes, however, people are very clear about the exact qualification they want or need and how their skills and knowledge directly relate to that qualification. In these cases, individuals are able to use the standards or expectations of the qualifications themselves to develop their profiles; they do not necessarily need to do such a complete review of their past experiences and accomplishments as someone who is less clear. (Chapter 5 covers this possibility.)

Imagine, for example, if Helen had wanted to receive a qualification in a secretarial subject or even a business studies area. She probably would have focused primarily on her work experience and used her skills and knowledge to meet the requirements of a particular secretarial or business qualification. On the other hand, suppose that she also was responsible for running a charity in her community; there might have been skills and

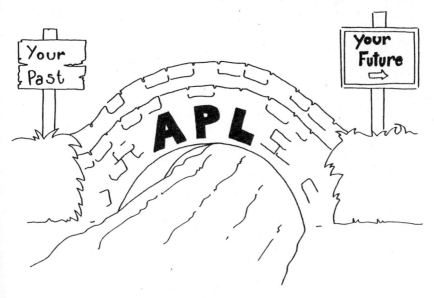

knowledge she could draw on from that experience as well which would have demonstrated her strengths.

In either case, the APL process can provide you with an important link between what you *have done* and what you *want to do*. You might think of APL as a valuable bridge, one that connects your past and your current life with your future direction. Let's begin at one end of the bridge and work our way across.

YOUR PAST

When you think about your past, what are all the things you have done? What have you learned? What have you enjoyed? Most of us have done so many things that it is difficult to know where to start.

Many people who go for a job prepare a curriculum vitae (CV) which is a brief description of their previous education and work history. If you have a CV, you may want to use it as a useful source of information. If you do not have one, you may want to develop one, just to get you started. You can use the format suggested below.

Do not worry if you have lots of blank spaces on your CV. Most people do. Your CV is just a sketch, not the three dimensional profile we're aiming for. Whatever its limitations or strengths, however, your CV provides a useful starting point for describing what you know and can do.

Next we want to add some detail to the sketch suggested by your CV. For this you will need to think about three things: your primary responsibilities, your day-to-day activities and then your accomplishments. Begin with the three forms shown in Figures 4.1, 4.2 and 4.3 but feel free to use additional paper as you need.

To help you get started, consider this example:

Tom is a computer software engineer. When he was describing himself, he listed some of his primary responsibilities as:

1. Analyse design problems.
2. Design software systems.
3. Implement software systems.
4. Contribute to developing new ideas within the team.
5. Supervise the work of three technical support staff.

For some of his day-to-day activities he listed:

1. Meet clients.
2. Carry out feasibility studies.
3. Run and attend meetings.
4. Review and correct outputs.

Name: _____

Address: _____

Day-time phone number: _____

Employment History

Job title   *Employer*   *Dates of Employment*

_____

_____

_____

Education and Training Background

Full-time education

                                        Dates

Institution   From   To

_____

_____

_____

Short or part-time training courses

                                        Dates

Institution   From   To

_____

_____

Qualifications or certificates

_____

_____

Hobbies, voluntary, leisure and domestic activities or special skills, eg, second language.

                                        Dates

Activity or place   From   To

Figure 4.1   *Curriculum Vitae*

5. Give staff assignments.
6. Check other people's work.
7. Monitor expenditures.

For some of his accomplishments he wrote:

1. Completed successful project to computerize local surgery.
2. Successfully changed computer system within my own organization.
3. Met budget targets.
4. Implemented monthly 'keeping in touch' meetings with staff.

Your forms may look very different from Tom's. But focusing on these three aspects of your activities – your responsibilities, your day-to-day activities and your accomplishments – will give you a clear focus for describing what you know and can do.

Are you surprised by what you see? Is it more than you expected? Hopefully you are beginning to get a good idea of all the things you know and can do.

For this exercise begin with your most recent job and work your way back. You will find that thinking about your current or most recent work will help you remember what you did in the past.

Job 1:
My title is (was):
My primary responsibilities are (were):

My daily activities include(d):

My main accomplishments are (were):

Job 2:
My title was:
My primary responsibilities were:

My day-to-day activities were:

My main accomplishments were:
Using a separate piece of paper, continue on for as many jobs as you like.

Figure 4.2   *Work history*

Activity 1

My title or role is (was):
My responsibilities are (were):

My day-to-day activities are (were):

My main accomplishments are (were):

Activity 2

My title or role was:
My responsibilities were:

My day-to-day activities were:

My main accomplishments were:

Using a separate sheet of paper, continue on with as many volunteer activities as you wish.

Figure 4.3   *Voluntary work*

On the form shown as Figure 4.3 you can include all those things that don't fall naturally into either of the other categories. For example, you might say that your hobby is collecting antiques, that you have a special interest in jazz music and that one of your special accomplishments has been caring for an elderly relative. This space is for you to use to describe all the things that make you the person you are.

My hobbies, interests and special accomplishments are:

These are some of the things I can do (or have done):

As appropriate:
My primary responsibilities are (were):

My day-to-day activities are (were):

My primary achievements are (were):

Figure 4.4   *Hobbies, interests and special accomplishments*

Now let's add some colour to this picture of you by highlighting what you:

1. enjoyed most;
2. feel most proud of; and
3. would like to have recognized towards a qualification.

Using a different coloured pen or pencil, go through each of the forms above, putting a star (*) next to each item you have listed – one for what you most enjoyed, another for what you are really proud of, and yet another for what you would like to have recognized towards a qualification.

Are there clusters emerging? Generally – but not always – people are most proud of things they have found challenging *and* that they have enjoyed; and they are often surprised at how many of these things relate to what they would like to be doing in the future, eg, the reason they want or need to receive recognition and qualifications.

YOUR CURRENT LIFE

Continuing on across the APL bridge, we need to take a closer look at your current life, in particular your *personal strengths*. Hopefully, in the forms you have just completed, you listed all the things you have done and no doubt are still doing. But largely these forms have captured your activities and accomplishments. To get a totally full picture of yourself, you need to look at the personal strengths you have that underpin all you know and can do. By recognizing your personal strengths it will be easier for you to determine the logical direction you wish to go in – and the qualification you will need to get there. You can use Checklist 4.1 to identify some of your personal strengths.

For all those things you ticked under 'most of the time', you should try to think of actual examples – as many as you can. Jot them down on a separate sheet of paper. Then go back and look at the three other forms you have completed. Are there things you can add from your Personal Strengths list to any of the forms that will make your Personal Profile more complete?

THE FUTURE

Now that you have a good picture of yourself, you need to think about what you want to do next in order to move to the other end of the APL bridge. What sort of qualification do you *really* want or need? What can you reasonably expect? How can you best use all you know and can do? Let's take a closer look at the qualifications available and what they could mean to you.

Checklist 4.1 *Your personal strengths*

Put a tick underneath the phrase that best describes you.

	Most of the time	Seldom
1. I work to improve things.		
2. I decide what needs to be done and how to do it.		
3. I compare what I set out to do with what I actually did.		
4. I respond to the needs of other people.		
5. I get along well with others.		
6. I get people to work together.		
7. I present a positive image.		
8. I have a sense of purpose in what I do.		
9. I deal constructively with my own emotions and pressures.		
10. I take responsibility for what I learn and do.		
11. I get information and use it.		
12. I come up with ideas and use them.		
13. I make decisions.		

As we said in earlier chapters, there are many different options available to you and times are changing so much that you may find you have a lot of choice in selecting an appropriate qualification. You will need to consider what you want from the APL centre you select in order to know how best to use the personal profile you have just developed. Whether your APL centre is a college of further or higher education, a polytechnic, university or an employer, all APL centres offer a range of qualifications.

One way to think about setting a qualification target for yourself is to think about the value of each type of qualification and what it could mean for you.

Selecting a qualification, course or training programme for which you want credit or recognition is the second step in the APL process.

Vocational qualifications

In general there are two sorts of vocational qualifications. One type generally prepares you for work and the other reflects your level of competence within work. Either type can serve as a stepping stone to higher level qualifications and new job prospects.

You may already be familiar with the type that generally prepares people for work. Examples of these traditional vocational qualifications include:

- BTEC Certificate in Business Studies;
- City and Guilds Certificate in Motor Vehicles;
- RSA Diploma in Office Procedures;
- SCOTVEC National Certificate in Catering.

These qualifications are generally earned at the end of a particular course of study, but increasingly the awarding bodies are introducing opportunities to enable more people to obtain them based on what they already know and can do.

Increasingly too, many of the awarding bodies are converting these traditional qualifications into NVQs or SVQs – reflecting the added importance of not just doing well in a course but of doing a good job in the world of work too.

NVQs and SVQs represent the second type of qualification, those that verify the skills, knowledge and abilities a person has demonstrated in the workplace. Hundreds of NVQs and SVQs are being developed, each designed to represent various levels of responsibility a person might hold in the workplace. Appendix 2 will give you a good idea of all the areas in which NVQs and SVQs are either available or are being developed.

It is important to add that many employers are also making NVQs and SVQs available to their employees. If you are employed, you may want to ask your employer if he or she is planning to make these qualifications available to you. If they are planned – or are already in place – you will have significant training and assessment opportunities available to you, one option of which may be APL.

APL is being encouraged in both types of qualifications, although as we shall see in the next chapter, NVQs and SVQs lend themselves very well to people with work experience and varied backgrounds because the expectations of each qualification is so clearly stated.

Degrees

There are many different kinds of degrees. The most common ones are the Bachelor of Arts (BA) and the Bachelor of Science (BSc). These are usually awarded after three or four years of study at a polytechnic or university.

Although most degrees at this level are not strictly speaking vocational qualifications, many different occupations require them. Some of these include: teaching, social work professionals, professional engineers, architects, psychologists, scientists, medical and para-medical professionals, legal and accountancy professionals, etc. In addition, degrees often help people to get management and other types of jobs not specific to the particular content of a degree course.

In the past most people entering a polytechnic or university had to have so many 'A' levels or 'H' grades. This is not so true today. Increasingly people, particularly adults, are being admitted through APL, personal interviews or other alternative means. So just because you lack 'A' levels or a vocational qualification, do not be discouraged about trying for a degree if you think that is what you want or need.

One final word about post-graduate degrees. Generally these are earned by people who have already been awarded a BA or BSc. They usually divide into two broad categories. Many are about research and the award of a Master of Philosophy (M. Phil.) or a Ph.D. means that an individual has demonstrated strong research skills. Other post-graduate degrees reflect more 'taught' courses related to specific occupational areas such as chemical engineering, law, or management.

At this point you may feel you have so many choices that it is difficult to begin. But, as we shall see in the next section, help is at hand! Don't be discouraged.

SUPPORT AT YOUR APL CENTRE

If you have progressed this far and have filled in all the forms and decided on a qualification or at least an area of interest, you have completed the first two steps of the APL process. But if you are like most people, you may want to talk through these matters and get some feedback from someone with experience in APL and the maze-like world of qualifications – if just to make sure you are on the right track. The logical place to do this is at your nearby APL centre.

WHAT YOU CAN EXPECT

When you go to your APL centre, you can expect to receive a lot of support and help. The centre may offer you an opportunity to attend a briefing or information session lasting from one to three hours. There you will learn about the APL process as it is offered by that centre. You will be encouraged to ask questions and in most instances will be given a lot of information about how long it may take, the range of services offered by the centre and fees. You may also be given an application or enrolment form to complete which will ask for information not unlike that you have already prepared earlier in this chapter.

At the briefing session you also may meet other people who share your interest in understanding what APL has to offer. You may find it reassuring to learn how many others have the same types of questions and concerns you have.

Following this briefing session, you will most likely have an opportunity to meet a trained APL adviser. Your adviser will be your main link with the centre and will help you through each stage of your APL work.

THE ROLE OF THE ADVISER

Your adviser will serve a number of different roles on your behalf. It is important to understand these different roles so that you can make good use of the opportunities presented to you. First and foremost your adviser will be your *advocate*, the person who helps you put your best foot forward. But to be your advocate, the adviser will have to get to know you – understand what you want out of APL, the centre and yourself. He or she will want to discuss your goals and help you to clarify them if necessary. He or she will want to understand a bit about your past – your relevant experiences – and provide you with sound information that will enable you to make your own decisions.

To fulfil this role, you generally will meet your adviser once, twice, or maybe more. In the process of the meeting the adviser will make sure that you:

- understand the APL process as it is offered at that centre;
- have objectives that the centre can actually help you achieve;
- select an appropriate qualification;
- develop a personal profile that will allow you to draw fully on all you know and can do;
- receive information about any workshops or group sessions that are available; and
- have your questions answered.

If you have a reading, or other, disability, your adviser as advocate also will work with you to find satisfactory alternative routes to help you progress through the APL process.

Another role your adviser can fulfil is that of *information gatherer*. As you have already read, there are so many changes occurring in the world of education and training that it is difficult to keep up with them all. Your adviser, however, should be able to cut through the red tape (at least some of it) to help you get the information you need. To be fair, however, advisers are human: they do not and cannot know everything there is to know. But most of them will be eager to help you in your search for information as best they can.

Also during all the various APL steps, your adviser will be a *record keeper.* Part of his or her professional responsibility is to keep clear and accurate records about each APL candidate. So do not be surprised if your APL adviser takes a lot of notes during your meetings. This is part of his or her job. On the other hand, it is your right to know what has been written about you. At the end of each meeting you and your adviser should review what has been discussed and decided. You should both have a clear idea of the outcomes and your respective responsibilities.

Lastly, your adviser will try to be a good *motivator.* In a way, this is part of being a good advocate, but it does entail a bit more. Most APL programmes require candidates to complete an Action or Assessment Plan. These plans are an agreement between you and the centre regarding what you are each going to do as part of your commitment to earn credit and qualifications through APL. Your adviser will want to help you follow your plan and reach your objectives. He or she will offer encouragement and respond to your questions when you are stuck. He or she will also be willing to talk through any problems you may encounter during your APL work.

WHAT THE APL ADVISER IS NOT

Most APL advisers are not therapists, social workers, or psychologists. They are not professionally qualified to help you solve major life problems, although most of them could probably help you find any such help should you need or want it.

Their function is basically that of a mentor or guide, someone you can lean on both to understand and work through the APL process. In later chapters we will talk more about the role of the adviser as you progress through the remaining steps of the APL process.

MOVING ON

As we have seen in this chapter, the first two steps of APL require you to make many decisions – about your past, your current life and your future. Whether you decide to develop your own profile and select a qualification on your own, you should by now at least be thinking about locating an APL centre to work with. It may well be that by the time you finish reading and using this book, you will be a lot further along the APL path than your adviser might expect. This could save you signficant time – and possibly money – allowing you to get the credit and qualifications you need more quickly.

Chapter 5

Do I Know Enough?

The next step in the APL process asks you to match your strengths with the requirements of the qualification, course or training programme you have selected. In this chapter we will take a close look at the nature of these requirements and how you can best use them to continue your APL work.

When most people begin the APL process, they usually ask themselves more than once, 'Do I know enough? Can I really do what will be expected? How will I know what I'm supposed to know and do, anyway?' No matter how many times people write out and think about all their strengths, until they can know and understand exactly what will be expected of them, they wonder whether or not they will be successful. Most APL candidates find that once they are familiar with the requirements or standards of their chosen qualification, course or training programme, however, they can save themselves a lot of unnecessary worry. So this chapter is about easing your mind – as well as helping you progress with your APL work.

USING STANDARDS

WHAT STANDARDS ARE

Generally speaking a 'standard' is a point of reference that states what has to be achieved or surpassed. For example, during the Olympics we often hear of the standard set by a particular team or individual. The record is there as a target to be achieved or surpassed by other athletes.

In qualifications the word 'standards' refers to the requirements or specifications set out within a given qualification, course or training programme. They spell out what an individual must know and be able to do before he or she can be awarded credit towards the particular qualification, course or training programme. Unlike the standards set in the Olympics, however, these standards do not pit one person against another. Rather, the standards are set so that each individual will have the same target – to reach or surpass.

Not so many years ago, few of us knew what was really expected of us to pass a test or examination. Even if we studied very hard, there was always an element of guesswork about whether we had learned the right things. Today, a lot of that guesswork is being removed from qualifications, courses and training programmes. People are being given the standards – or requirements – to help them learn and to allow them to see what they have achieved as they continue to learn. To give you an idea of what a standard is, consider the following example.

If you were asked whether or not you could write letters, in all probability you would answer 'yes'. If you were then asked whether you could write business and friendly letters, you might say 'yes' to the friendly letters and 'not so sure' about the business letters.

Since there are so many different kinds of business letters, you might want to know what was meant by the term 'business letters' before you answered. For example, you might well be able to write a letter to the gas board questioning their most recent reading of your meter, but you might feel less able to write a formal letter of agreement such as sometimes exists between a builder and a subcontractor. Both are business letters, but each requires a different set of skills and knowledge.

The point is, of course, that the more you know what is expected or meant by certain words, the better able you are to answer questions about whether you know or can do something. This is the basic idea behind giving people the standards and helping them to use them to figure out for themselves what they know and can do.

Let's take the example one step further. Suppose, after reviewing all the descriptions, you have said that you could write a range of different types of business letters. The next set of questions might be about how well you actually prepare them. For example, you might be asked whether or not all of your letters are:

- grammatically correct;
- without spelling errors;
- formatted properly;
- legible.

and so forth. This type of information spells out the exact requirements – the standards – to give you a clear idea of what is expected in each of the letters you prepare. It describes in detail what would be a desirable outcome in all the letters you write: that they reflect the generally accepted standard of a good business letter.

Standards, in the context in which you will be using them in your APL work, describe *activities* you will be expected to perform, and let you know the minimum level of performance acceptable to an assessor.

Standards, then can help you in a number of ways during the APL process. They can help you:

1. Match your strengths with the requirements of the qualification, course, or training programme you have selected.
2. Remember things you know and can do that you may not have included in your Personal Profile.
3. See where you need to improve.
4. Develop your claim to credit for use at the next step in the APL process.

Let's take each of these in turn.

MATCHING WHAT YOU KNOW AND CAN DO WITH THE STANDARDS

Because standards spell out what is expected of each individual, they serve as excellent markers against which you can match your own skills and knowledge. Both NVQs and SVQs are based on standards of performance in the workplace. Although other qualifications are also based on standards, it is useful to get an idea of standards by looking at NVQs and SVQs because, for the most part, they are so clearly presented. Let's take a close look at some.

NVQs and SVQs
NVQs and SVQs are written in a particular way to make them readily understandable. They are divided into three main sections called Units, Elements of Competence, and Performance Criteria. Although these words may seem off-putting at first, if you decide to acquire an NVQ or SVQ, they will quickly become part of your normal vocabulary (although it may seem hard to believe at the moment).

Unit: simply put, a unit describes a *role* which is part of a job that a person might be expected to do in the workplace. It has a specific title which describes that role. A number of units put together make up a full qualification.

Elements of competence: within each unit there are elements of competence. These are the *activities* that a competent person would be expected to do in the workplace. There may be two to eight elements of competence within a unit, that is, two to eight main activities that are required to perform that job.

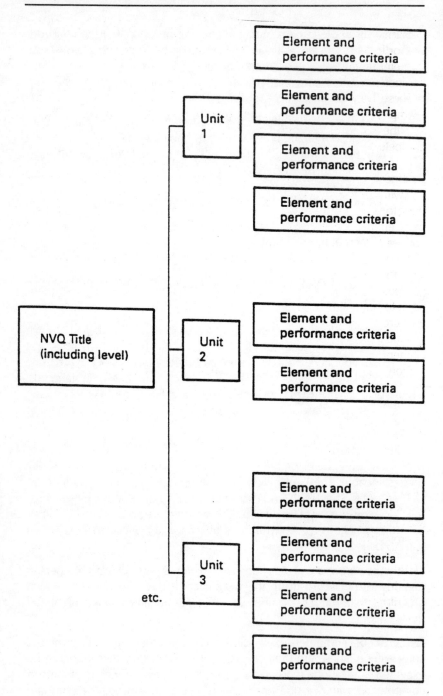

Figure 5.1 *Structure of new qualifications*

Performance criteria: performance criteria provide information on *how well* or in what way the activity is to be performed. They provide the basis for determining whether or not the person is performing the activity in a competent manner.

These new qualifications specify other important information too, for example, the knowledge and understanding you will be expected to know and the *range* of contexts in which you may be asked to apply your competence.

In most cases, the range of contexts will be expressed as 'range statements'. These will be particularly helpful to you in that they can provide you with detailed information about the nature of evidence you will need to bring forward. But for our purposes, however, we will focus on the use of the units, elements of competence and performance criteria – just to give you an idea of what these new qualifications are all about.

If a person is able to perform all the elements of competence in keeping with the performance criteria, he or she is said to be 'occupationally competent' and entitled to credit for that unit. Perhaps the most important point to be made about this new structure of qualifications is that you can earn credit for *each* unit, one at a time. You do not have to try for the whole qualification at one time. Figure 5.1 shows the relationship between units, elements of competence and performance criteria.

Don't worry if this still seems a bit confusing – it's not easy at first. You may need to take a look at a few examples before you can really get the idea. The example that follows is taken from the National Vocational Qualification (NVQ) in Business Administration – Level II (Financial). It is available from the RSA Examinations Board.

Within this qualification there are 15 units. These include:

Communicating Information	Providing information to
Data Processing	customers/clients
Stock Handling	Storing and supplying information
Mail Handling	Information processing
Reprographics	Processing payments
Liaising with callers and colleagues	Processing documents relating
Health and Safety	to goods and services
Creating and maintaining	Processing payroll
business relationships	Maintaining financial records

Each one of these unit titles suggests something a person might do as part of his or her job, for example, handle stock, process payments, maintain financial records, and so forth. Some also suggest responsibilities that relate to all of the others, for example, communicate information and create and maintain business relationships. A person would have to demonstrate competence – meet the standard – in all of these units to get this National

Vocational Qualification (NVQ). However, it is worth repeating that one of the strengths of NVQs is that you can get credit for just one unit at a time.

Within each of the units are the different activities – the elements of competence – that you would be expected to do. For example in *creating and maintaining business relationships*, there are two elements of competence. These are:

1. Create and maintain professional relationships with other members of staff.
2. Create and maintain professional relationships with customers and clients.

By contrast, the unit called *information processing* contains three elements of competence.

1. Process records in a database.
2. Process information in spreadsheets.
3. Access and print hard copy reports, summaries and documents.

Again, elements of competence describe the *activities* you would be expected to perform as part of your job, but they don't tell you *how* you would be expected to perform, do they? You need to look at the performance criteria to get that information.

The performance criteria for *create and maintain professional relationships with other members of staff* include:

- Requests from colleagues within the jobholder's responsibility are actioned promptly and willingly, where possible.
- Essential information is passed on to colleagues promptly and accurately.
- Assistance, when required, is requested politely.
- Effective and mutually beneficial arrangements are made regarding division of work and joint responsibilities.
- Significant difficulties in working relationships are discussed, resolved or reported accurately to an appropriate authority.

The performance criteria for *information processing* look like this:

- Information is correctly accessed by document/record/file as directed.
- All printed output conforms to specification.
- Documents are correctly collated and distributed, as directed.
- Security and confidentiality of information is always maintained.
- Faults/failures are identified and reported promptly.
- Operating, safety and maintenance procedures are followed at all times.

Are you beginning to get the idea of standards? Unlike many traditional qualifications, NVQs and SVQs specify very clearly what you will be expected to do and know. They allow you, as part of the APL process, to match what you *already* know and can do with what is expected.

Once you know what qualification you want, your APL centre will give you an exact set of the standards so you can begin to compare what you know and can do with what is expected. No longer will you need to 'read the examiner's mind' to figure out what will be expected of you to gain the qualification you need or want. You will be able to look at the requirements – the standards – of each unit and decide whether or not you know and can do what is expected.

CHECKLISTS

Sometimes, of course, what seems clear to one person, does not seem so clear to another. And sometimes the language used in standards seems a bit too formal or not part of every-day speech. For example, most of us don't use the word 'jobholder' (as appears above) very often – if at all! Most of us would probably use another word like worker, employee, or even person. But since the standards of NVQs and SVQs are intended for use at the national level, the words used must apply to large numbers of people working in a great variety of settings. For this reason, the words are not always the most natural-sounding ones.

So to help APL candidates actually *use* the standards, many APL centres develop checklists. The checklists are written to reflect the basic idea behind the standards and are generally written in plain English. Every attempt is made to relate the likely experiences of individuals to the standards so that it becomes even easier to determine whether or not what you know and can do matches the standards.

Checklists take many different forms. For example, in a recent BTEC qualification in Business Studies, APL candidates were asked to put a tick next to all the elements of competence that applied to what they could do. The elements of competence were presented as straightforward activities. Each checklist began with 'I am able to . . .' and candidates were asked to tick the ones they could do.

    __1. Create a database file on commercially available software for recording, updating, manipulating and retrieving information.

    __2. Create a spreadsheet on commercially available software for recording, calculating and retrieving information.

    __3. Create documents using commercially available word-processing software.

___4. Access a commercial viewdata system to extract and print-out business information.

___5. Use commercially available software for specific business applications.

Other checklists, intended for similar purposes, can begin with different phrases such as 'have you . . .' or 'can you . . .' As you will note, however, these checklists relate only to the activities; they do not relate to the performance criteria.

Sometimes, APL candidates are asked to consider the performance criteria as well in checklists. Look at the example provided below based on a Health and Safety unit taken from the NVQ in Vehicle Engineering developed by Bus and Coach Training Limited. The element of competence reads: *Maintain personal safety and hygiene.*

The performance criteria in checklist form might read:

(a) Do you wear protective clothing?   Yes   No
   If yes, is it clean, undamaged and appropriately used at all times?   Yes   No

(b) Are your clothing, hair and body ornaments secured and covered as appropriate to the activity?   Yes   No

(c) Do you obtain, check and use relevant safety equipment?   Yes   No

(d) Can you identify the limitations on your natural senses when using safety equipment?   Yes   No
   If yes, do you make appropriate compensations in your actions?   Yes   No

The use of checklists, regardless of how they are prepared, are there for you to use, to help you match what you know and can do with the expectations of the qualification, course, or training programme for which you are seeking credit.

Other uses of the standards
Although the primary purpose behind the standards at this point in the APL process is to help you link your strengths with the requirements of the qualification, standards will be useful to you in a number of other ways as well. It may be worth making a note of these as you think about the overall purpose and benefits of APL.

1. Reviewing the standards, whether in checklist form or not, can remind you of things you know and can do that you have not included in your Personal Profile. Often people go back and modify their Personal Profiles as a result of using the standards. In truth, using the standards can provide you with an excellent opportunity to 'round out' your Profile – just as referring to your Profile can make it easier for you to use and relate to the standards.

2. Using the standards can also help you identify areas in which you need to improve. Although the main purpose of APL is to help you get the recognition and qualifications you want and need, the process can also help you to see what else you might want to learn, know or be able to do. More than one person who has completed the APL process has said, 'I never thought about my job in that way; I didn't realize that it was important to do that . . .'

Reviewing the standards and thinking about what you know and can do can highlight for you areas that you will want to develop. As has already been pointed out, one of the best things about APL and the new types of qualifications is that you do not need to do everything at once. You can earn credit for what you know and can do *now*. Then, when you are ready – when you feel you can tackle more units – you can go back and earn more credit or complete the entire qualification. In any given time period, you do not need to take on more than you can do comfortably.

3. Most important, using the standards will allow you to develop clear statements of what you hope to receive credit for. These 'claims to credit' as they are sometimes called, will allow your adviser and assessor(s) to see at a glance what you claim to know already and are able to do. As we will see in the next chapter, they will provide the framework by which you will complete the APL process.

Other qualifications and standards

In most of this chapter we have looked at the standards of NVQs and SVQs. But it is important to remember that standards are creeping into other qualifications too. Sometimes they are called by different names, for example, learning outcomes or learning attainments, but basically they provide similar types of information for you to use. Unlike NVQs and SVQs many of the standards or learning outcomes of other qualifications refer to the expected outcomes of a particular course or training programme. They are not based on performance at work but this does not mean that your work experience would not be highly relevant!

For example, City and Guilds (C&G) is piloting The Technological Baccalaureate in city technology colleges, further education colleges and schools. Even though it describes a particular course of study, this qualification is written in NVQ-like terms. For example, there are elements of competence, eg, *identify occasions and purposes requiring measurements and identify quantities to be measured*; and there are performance criteria, eg, *the purpose of measurement is clearly established or the degree of accuracy required (or possible) is identified*. The fact that it is written in this manner will make it a lot easier for you to determine (a) what you already know and can do and (b) what else you might have to learn to get the whole qualification.

Looking at another example, in a recent two-year project[1] a team of researchers investigated ways in which lecturers at polytechnics and universities could describe a number of degree courses in terms of expected learning outcomes. These learning outcomes, while also not linked specifically to performance in the workplace, were intended to describe what successful graduates should be able to know and do at the end of the course. They provide a varied mixture of skills, knowledge and personal strengths. For example, a few of the learning outcomes in design stated that:

Design graduates should be able to:

- Understand aspects of the law as it applies to design and designers.
- Plan a strategy which will lead to a design.
- Manipulate forms with a high degree of skill.
- Explain, justify and present design solutions.
- Delegate tasks.
- Critically reflect on practice.

By expressing learning outcomes such as these, polytechnics and universities are also beginning to provide new avenues for people to seek easier admission, credit and other forms of recognition for what they already know and can do.

Although not yet widespread, the introduction of learning outcomes in higher education is a step in the right direction, allowing more people to make better use of their time and effort in degree courses. If you are interested in obtaining a degree, you will want to find out if the polytechnic or university of your choice has developed learning outcomes or other guidance that will help you progress through the system more easily and quickly – and receive the recognition and credit you deserve.

WHAT YOU CAN EXPECT FROM YOUR APL CENTRE

At your APL centre you can expect to receive sets of the standards or learning outcomes of the qualification in which you are interested. Your adviser may give you the standards as they are or you might receive them in checklist format. In either case you should ask for them, if you are not automatically given them, and request time to review them carefully.

You may need to look at a range of qualifications in a particular area to make sure that you are aiming at the right level to get the qualification that best reflects what you know and can do. For example, we have talked about

[1] UDACE (1991) *What Can Graduates Do?* UDACE, Leicester.

the range of qualifications available – from vocational qualifications to degrees. But even within NVQs, for example, there are four levels of qualifications:

> LEVEL 1 reflects work activities that are often routine, predictable and supervised.
>
> LEVEL 2 reflects work activities that are generally considered to be more demanding than Level 1 and often involve greater individual responsibility.
>
> LEVEL 3 reflects activities in skilled areas that often involve a broad range of activities, including many that are complex and non-routine. Often at this level, the person would be expected to have some supervisory responsibility.
>
> LEVEL 4 reflects work activities in complex, technical and professional areas and generally includes supervision and management responsibility.

If you are aiming for an NVQ, an SVQ, or a traditional qualification, you may need help in sorting out the one(s) best for you. By looking at a range of standards or checklists you and your adviser will be able to identify the one(s) that best fit what you know and can do *and* what you will need to do to complete the entire qualification.

So the standards or learning outcomes can be used in different ways:

1. They can help you identify the qualification that will best suit you.
2. They can help you match what you know and can do with the expectations of the qualification, course or training programme you have selected.
3. They can help you remember things you may have omitted from your Personal Profile.
4. They can help you identify new things to learn.
5. They can help you develop your claims to credit which will form the basis of the rest of your APL work.

It is to this last purpose – so essential to your success – that we shall now turn our attention.

Chapter 6

How Will I Prove It?

Once you have matched your skills, knowledge and abilities with the standards, you are ready to progress to the fourth step of the APL process, proving what you know and can do. In some ways, this is the most challenging part of the process and many people find it the most satisfying.

In this chapter we shall look at many of the different ways you can prove you meet the standards of the qualification you are working towards. A number of worksheets have also been provided to help you begin to organize your proof when you are ready. But first, let's pick up where we left off in Chapter 5 – with your claims to credit.

USING YOUR CLAIM TO CREDIT FORMS

The claim to credit forms provided by your APL centre will allow you to list exactly what you are seeking credit for. If you are hoping to get an NVQ, you will list the units and elements of competence; if you are hoping for another type of qualification, you will provide other descriptions of what you will be seeking to have accredited. Sometimes the checklists you complete will serve as your claim to credit forms and sometimes you may have to complete a summary form, often called an assessment or learning contract. By whatever name, it is still your statement of what you want to receive credit for.

In most cases, you will also be asked to think about and list the ways in which you think you can prove what you know and can do. For example, if you were claiming elements of competence in computer programming,

Checklist 6.1 and 2 *Claim to credit*

CLAIM TO CREDIT CHECKLIST

SCOTVEC Module 61008: Public Speaking

I am able to:	X	Evidence
Plan and prepare for a public presentation	X	Outline and notes of two presentations I did. One for the Chamber of Commerce; another related to my work.
Deliver a public presentation	X	Programmes showing me as a speaker. Audiotape of one presentation. Video tape of the other.

CLAIM TO CREDIT CHECKLIST

SCOTVEC Module 61013: Interviewing Skills

I am able to:	X	Evidence
Plan an interview which is appropriate to purpose	X	Correspondence between me and housing association confirming purpose and expected outcomes of interview. Notes I used to develop each draft of the interview.
Conduct an interview employing interpersonal skills and appropriate questioning techniques	X	Audio-tape of three interviews.
Evaluate the results of the interview in relation to its purpose	X	Report I prepared for the housing association. Letter from the association thanking me for work well done!

---

you would probably want to use some of your programs as proof. If you were a journalist, you would no doubt use a range of articles you had written. If you were a vocalist, you might prepare tapes of your singing. If you raised money for a charity, you might bring in some of the publicity material you had produced. If you were a metal worker you might identify components you had made and so forth.

In almost all cases you would be encouraged to list the best examples you had that would help prove that you could meet the standards or requirements of the qualification you were seeking. Clearly, the more closely linked your proof is to what is asked for in the standards, the stronger your chances are of being successful.

Look at the examples in Checklist 6.1 and 2 to see how one candidate completed her checklists and began to identify her proof.

In completing these claim to credit forms, the candidate was saying to her APL centre, 'This is what I am able to do and this is how I will prove it to you'. You will have the same opportunity – and responsibility. The rest of this chapter will tell you how you can go about it.

EVIDENCE

'Evidence' is the term used to describe the proof you will present that you really know and can do what you claim. There are many different kinds of evidence and you will want to make sure that the evidence you use to prove your competence really does just that. In collecting or generating evidence, you will be led by the requirements of the qualification you are seeking, but you will also want to draw heavily from your Personal Profile. At this point, your Personal Profile is a bit like a personal safe – it contains your most valuable assets.

IDENTIFYING EVIDENCE

Keeping in mind that you will want to present the strongest possible evidence you can, there are a number of principles you should keep in mind. These principles are the same as those the assessors will be applying as they review your evidence at the next step in the APL process. So it is important that you think about and apply these principles to your own situation.

In general evidence falls into two categories: direct and indirect.

Direct evidence includes anything that you yourself have produced. Some examples include reports you may have written, garments you may have sewn, drawings you may have created, engines you may have repaired, spreadsheets you may have produced – anything that is the direct result of your effort.

Indirect evidence includes anything *about* you that tells or describes what you have done. Some examples include newspaper articles about your accomplishments, letters from past or current employers or associates, photographs of a piece of furniture (or anything else) you may have built, certificates from previous training courses, etc.

Most often, direct evidence is considered stronger, more representative of what you know and can do than indirect evidence. But most APL candidates find that they use a combination of evidence to prove their claims to credit. Before we move on, you may want to think about the competences, skills, knowledge or personal strengths that you are hoping to receive credit for. Can you identify a few examples of direct and indirect evidence from your own accomplishments? Take a minute to jot them down here.

Checklist 6.3   *Examples of evidence*

Direct	Indirect

Once you have identified some examples of evidence, you will want to think about the four basic ideas or principles that your assessor will be using to judge your evidence. You will then want to make sure that you identify and select evidence in keeping with these principles. Simply stated the four basic principles are:

1. Relevance
2. Authenticity
3. Currency
4. Sufficiency

We'll take a close look at each one so that you will be able to develop the strongest evidence you can.

1. *Relevance*: This refers to how clearly your evidence relates to the standards. The more closely your evidence meets the requirements of the qualification, the easier it will be for the assessor to confirm your competence. The example of John may serve to illustrate this principle.

John was a professional trainer who wanted to prove his competence to deliver training. The elements of competence said he had to be able to *plan* a training programme, *design* the programme in keeping with the requirements of the people to be trained, actually *run the training course* and *evaluate* his effectiveness. He believed that his evidence could prove that he had carried out each of these activities in keeping with the specified performance criteria.

To support his claims to credit, John was able to bring forward

(a) his draft plans for the training event and the final programme;

(b) several pieces of correspondence that showed he had actually negotiated the programme with the people who had hired him to run the training event;

(c) a video tape taken during the training event, showing him delivering the training; and

(d) a copy of the feedback form he had prepared along with a summary of what the participants said about the event, using the form.

Each of these examples of evidence was *relevant* to what John was expected to prove. (Please note that most APL programmes use the word 'validity' to describe relevance but don't be misled by this technical word. If you think about the 'relevance' of your evidence, more than likely you will be on the right track.)

2. *Authenticity*: This refers to whether or not the evidence you present is really your work. You will want to make sure beyond a reasonable doubt that your evidence actually reflects your work. Again, an example will be helpful.

Sara worked as a clerk in a small department store. She wanted to earn the NVQ Retail Certificate, Level 2. One of the elements of competence said she should be able to create and set up displays. Although Sara helped create and set up displays, she did not do the work by herself all the time. She and the other members of the staff often worked as a team. The evidence Sara included to support her claim to credit included:

(a) a range of photographs showing different displays she had helped to create and set up;

(b) a brief personal report that she wrote that provided details of her contribution to each of the displays; and

(c) a letter from her employer who described her work and verified that she could perform all the necessary functions by herself or in a team situation.

In combination, Sara was able to prove the authenticity of her work even though she often worked in a team.

3. *Currency*: This refers to how recent your evidence is. You will need to remember that although you may be using evidence from your past accomplishments, your assessor(s) will want to make sure that you can do what you claim you can *today*. For this reason, while most candidates draw on evidence from the past, sometimes they need to generate more recent examples. The example of Sean below provides a good illustration.

For as many years as he could remember Sean liked to 'fool around' with cars and over the years worked on a number of rally cars. He was in the army for six years and during that time served as a mechanic. When he left the army eight years ago, he got a job in the security industry. He did not enjoy this work particularly and wanted to get back to working with his hands. He decided to become a qualified mechanic using APL. To that end Sean was able to bring forward:

(a) his certificates of training from the army (some of which were now 14 years old);

(b) various photographs of his previous rally cars; and

(c) his current rally car which he was able to drive to his APL centre.

Sean's evidence addressed the matter of currency very directly. His various army certificates confirmed his training, the photographs supported his on-going interest, and of course his current rally car provided a good indication of his current competence. As you can see, not all APL evidence needs to be on paper!

4. *Sufficiency*: This refers to the amount and diversity of evidence you need to bring forward. You need to have enough ... but not so much that you overwhelm your assessor. Although you will be guided very much by the standards, you will need to choose your evidence carefully. The case of Liz provides a good example of this.

Liz was a musician. She had taken piano lessons when she was young and over the years had taught herself basic composition and arranging skills. She composed a number of pieces for community groups and was frequently called on to supervise rehearsals and the performance of her compositions. When she decided to earn a qualification in music, she had stacks of things to select from. She had to read the learning outcome statements of the qualification in which she was interested very carefully in order to select her best work. Eventually she chose:

(a) three of her original compositions, each quite different from the other;

(b) two different arrangements of the same piece;

(c) the rehearsal schedules for four compositions; and

(d) a range of newspaper articles that reviewed her work.

Selecting just the right amount and type of evidence is tricky. But if you use the standards of the qualification and think about your best examples, you will probably provide sufficient evidence.

These four concepts then – relevance, authenticity, currency and sufficiency – should be your guideposts in selecting your best evidence. You may want to use the worksheet shown in Figure 6.1 to develop the lists of evidence you can bring forward. Use one for each portion of the qualification you are seeking. (Figure 6.1 has been prepared for use with NVQs or SVQs but you can modify it to suit your own needs.) Be sure to refer to your Personal Profile to stimulate your thoughts.

Qualification name _____

Unit _____ Element of Competence _____

Type of Evidence	Available	Needs to be created	Received/ Developed
_____	_____	_____	_____
_____	_____	_____	_____
_____	_____	_____	_____
_____	_____	_____	_____

Unit _____ Element of Competence _____

Type of Evidence	Available	Needs to be created	Received/ Developed
_____	_____	_____	_____
_____	_____	_____	_____
_____	_____	_____	_____
_____	_____	_____	_____

Figure 6.1 *Evidence worksheet*

To complete the worksheet, put the name of the qualification you are seeking, the unit and element of competence titles and list the type of evidence you need to bring forward. If you already have the evidence – if it is readily available – put a tick under 'Available'. If it needs to be developed or created, put a tick there. When you actually have it, put a tick in the last column! Feel free to make as many copies of the worksheet as you need.

At this point, you still may have questions about the nature of evidence. We shall address some of the more frequently asked ones and hope they cover at least a few of yours.

What about these letters from my employer? What are they and how do I get them?
Letters from your employers, whether past or present, can provide valuable information about you. These letters are often called 'letters of validation' because they serve to validate or verify what you know and can do.

Letters of reference or recommendation rarely fulfil the validation role because most often they simply provide a few facts or generalities about an individual. In contrast, letters of validation must describe what you did/do, under what circumstances, when, for how long, and how well you performed.

Under ideal conditions, the people you ask to write on your behalf should be familiar not just with what you know and can do but also with the standards or the requirements of the qualification you are hoping to earn. For this reason, they may need some help from you. You may want to use Figure 6.2 to develop your own letters of request.

What about letters from other people, not just employers? Can they write on my behalf?
Anyone who is familiar with what you know and can do can write on your behalf. For example, a person who runs a small business may ask his or her accountant to write; people who are involved in charities might ask their colleagues or a regional coordinator to write; even satisfied customers or clients can write on your behalf. Anyone *can* write but you will need to consider the strength or weight of that person's testimony about you. Will it truly support what you know and can do? Will the person be viewed as credible by your assessors? Only you can answer these questions but you will no doubt want to discuss these matters with your adviser. One word of advice: generally letters from family members are not recommended.

What do I do if my evidence is confidential?
Many people who go through the APL process have good examples of evidence that they cannot use for reasons of confidentiality or security. This does not mean that they cannot earn credit for what they know and can do.

4 January 1992

Mrs Nancy Robinson
Ace Manufacturing Company
Newtown N2 3LL

Dear Mrs Robinson,

As we discussed on the telephone, I am writing to ask you for a letter on my behalf for a special programme at Smith College of Further Education. As part of their accreditation of prior learning (APL) programme, I am hoping to earn credits towards a national qualification in catering for learning I acquired outside the college classroom. Your letter will help me provide evidence that what I already know and can do is equal to many of the requirements of the qualification. I have included a copy of these requirements for your reference.

Following the recommendations of the College, I would like your letter to include the following:

1. A description of my position as assistant head of the canteen between 1985 and 1990. This should include a brief mention of the responsibilities I assumed and some of my main accomplishments.
2. A mention of your relationship to me, for example, that you were my immediate supervisor, and the situations under which you observed me or evaluated my work.
3. An indication of the skills, knowledge and abilities you believe I possess. (You may want to refer to the requirements of the qualification which I have enclosed.)
4. And lastly, a statement indicating how well you think I met the overall job role. I would appreciate your sending your letter on company stationary to my adviser at the college. His name is Joseph Reading and his address is as follows (insert address). I would like this letter to reach him by 16 February, if at all possible. (Allow your letter writer at least one month from the date you write your request letter.)

Thank you very much for agreeing to write this letter on my behalf. As I am sure you are aware, earning a qualification at this point in my life is very important to me.

Should you have questions, please let me know.

Thank you once again.

Yours sincerely,

Your Name

Figure 6.2 *Sample request letter*

Rather they must work with their adviser to develop alternative ways of generating the evidence. Possible examples include:

1. deleting the confidential portions;

2. seeing if the assessor can view the information at the location at which it exists;
3. developing similar material that does not contain the confidential or secure information, as such; and
4. undergoing a different type of assessment as is described in the next chapter.

Do I have to submit originals of all my work or can I use photocopies?
Most paper evidence can be photocopied, as long as the material is still legible and reflects your work. Other things such as sweets you have cooked or furniture you have built will have to come in their original form! Often, though, authenticated photographs of your work can be used too.

Can I use certificates or other qualifications as evidence?
The answer to this question is sometimes 'yes' and sometimes 'no'. It will depend very much on what the certificate or qualification is for, when you earned it, what it reflects about what you know and can do, and, most important, how it relates to your claim to credit. You will probably need to seek advice from your adviser on this matter.

Do I always need to prepare a personal report?
It is not always necessary to do this, although a report can be useful if your other evidence is not too strong. A personal report is a description of the activities and functions you have carried out that relate to the standards you are trying to meet. You might also want to include reflections on your actions, for example, how you planned something, why you made certain decisions, what you would have done differently in retrospect, what knowledge you needed to apply, etc. A personal report allows you to describe yourself as you want to be seen.

In most cases your personal report will be used with other assessments as are described in the next chapter. It is worth adding that many centres do not require a personal report. Much of the information you might convey in a written report, you may be able to convey in conversation with your assessor. Once again, your adviser will provide you with the best guidance.

What if I don't have any evidence – direct or indirect – but know that I can meet the standards?
This is frequently the case with people who have moved around a great deal, people who work in occupations in which there are no specific products (like care or social service occupations), or people who have acquired the necessary skills and knowledge basically on their own (like local history buffs). If you feel that you are in a similar situation, you will need to discuss with your adviser the various ways in which you could prove your competence, even without any concrete evidence. You may be asked to prepare a personal report which would allow you to relate your skills,

knowledge and abilities to the standards. This document might then serve as the basis for other assessments such as are described in the next chapter.

Will I need to have a separate piece of evidence for each element of competence or each part of the qualification I am seeking?
You will be glad to know that there is no expectation that you will have a single, separate piece of evidence for each of the elements of competence or individual parts of the qualification you are seeking. Almost all the things people produce relate to more than one portion of the standard or qualification. For this reason you may find that one or two pieces of evidence will relate to several different areas of your competence. Again, you will need to be led by the standards but your adviser will provide help with this issue as well.

How long will it take to get my evidence together?
Regrettably there is no single answer to this question because there are so many factors to consider. For example, the number of units for which you are seeking credit, the amount and diversity of the evidence you have available and the amount of time you are prepared to give to your APL work will all influence the length of time it will take to collect or develop your evidence. The good news is, however, that with APL you have a lot more flexibility in completing the necessary requirements for a qualification than you do through more traditional routes.

Regardless of the amount of time it takes, there is no doubt that identifying and selecting your evidence will be the most challenging part of your APL work. Throughout each step in the process, you will want to:

- read the standards carefully and be guided by them as you develop your evidence;
- think through the four principles carefully;
- use your Personal Profile;
- develop worksheets for yourself so you can carefully monitor what you have and what you need; and
- discuss your problems of evidence with your adviser.

DEVELOPING YOUR PORTFOLIO OF EVIDENCE

Once you have collected or developed all the evidence you think you need, you will want to put it all together in a 'portfolio'. When most people hear the word portfolio they think of an art student's work or set of financial papers. In APL, however, the portfolio refers to the file in which you present all of the necessary information about yourself which will allow the assessor(s) to assess you. A portfolio includes several different items:

1. A cover page.
2. A table of contents.
3. A statement of what you are seeking to have accredited, eg, your claim to credit forms or a summary document such as an assessment contract.
4. A completed Personal Profile or detailed CV.
5. Cross-referencing forms.
6. The evidence itself.

We shall describe each one:

1. *A cover page*: This should contain your name, address, phone number, and name of your APL centre. Sometimes you will be asked to include your adviser's name and the date you actually submit your portfolio as well.

2. *A table of contents*: Just like a book or magazine, your table of contents should list the page numbers for each section of your portfolio.

3. *A statement of what you are seeking to have accredited*: Whether it is called a claim to credit form, assessment or learning contract, or some other name, you will be asked to produce a clear indication of each part of the qualification you are seeking to have accredited. Your APL centre will provide guidance and instruction about this section of the portfolio.

4. *A Personal Profile or detailed CV*: A completed Personal Profile, detailed CV or some other description of you will almost always be asked for in your portfolio. Such a document provides a full picture of you and helps to link your experiences and accomplishments with both the standards you have used to develop your evidence and the evidence itself.

5. *Cross-referencing forms*: These will enable you to indicate which pieces of evidence you are using to prove each competence you are claiming. They will also serve as the assessor's guide to your evidence. (The example in Appendix 4 provided by the Management Charter Initiative gives you an example to use.)

6. *The evidence itself*: Clearly, the evidence itself is the most important part of your portfolio. So you will want to make sure it is neatly presented and carefully numbered. You also will want to make sure that the numbers presented on your cross-referencing forms really do reflect the numbers you have assigned to each piece of evidence!

Lastly, unless something is totally self-explanatory, you may want to write a brief description or explanation of each piece of evidence and describe how it relates to the competence(s) you are claiming. This may make the assessor's job easier and serve to strengthen your claim even more.

You may want to use Checklist 6.4 to help you monitor your own progress as you work towards preparing your portfolio.[1]

Checklist 6.4 *For portfolio production*

Monitor your own progress by entering the date on which you complete each activity.	
Activity	*Date Completed*
■ Personal Profile completed	
■ Claim to credit forms or assessment contract completed	
■ Evidence identified	
■ Letters of validation requested (if used)	
■ Letters of validation received (if requested)	
■ All available direct and indirect evidence collected	
■ New evidence developed (if needed)	
■ Personal report prepared (if needed)	
■ Each piece of evidence numbered (including personal report)	
■ Cross-referencing forms filled in	
■ Brief descriptions of each piece of evidence prepared (as needed)	
■ Cover and table of contents written	
■ Portfolio collated	
■ Portfolio submitted	

A final word about your portfolio: it is your personal account of what you know and can do. It is also your statement of what you want or need to receive recognition, credit and/or a qualification for. For this reason you will want to make sure it is as good as you are! You should make sure that:

■ Your portfolio is neat and, if possible, typed.

[1] This checklist has been adapted from the checklist printed in Simosko (1991), *Crediting Competence Workbook*, page 124, published and used with the kind permission of the Management Charter Initiative.

- Your portfolio is error free and that the grammar, spelling and punctuation reflect good practice.
- Your portfolio is carefully bound so that bits and pieces cannot be lost or misplaced.
- Any items that do not fit neatly into your portfolio – like rally cars, sewn garments or machined metal! – are nonetheless numbered and then described in your portfolio.

SUBMITTING YOUR PORTFOLIO

The day you submit your portfolio will be an exciting day for you. You may also have a great sense of relief, even though you no doubt will realize that once your APL centre receives your portfolio that is the beginning of step 5, your actual assessment. We will turn our attention to the assessment process in the next chapter. For now though, it is important to remind you of what you can expect during *this* step in the APL process, proving what you know and can do.

WHAT YOU CAN EXPECT FROM YOUR APL CENTRE

Your APL centre will be prepared to give you a lot of help and support during this stage of your APL work. Not only will you have your adviser to turn to, but many centres offer a range of other services as well. Let us take a brief look at a few of these possibilities.

1. *Guide to portfolio production*: Many APL centres will have developed some sort of written guide to help you identify, select and develop your evidence, all leading to the production of your portfolio. They will also give you all the necessary forms they expect you to use. Some may even have produced a video detailing the process; and others may have some sample portfolios for you to review and refer to as you develop your own.

2. *Portfolio development workshops*: Increasingly APL centres are beginning to offer workshops to help people address issues related to evidence collection and portfolio production. These can be structured sessions which address specific topics or they can be more open-ended, with one of the advisers there to take questions from the group. You may have to pay for these sessions but if you are a person who finds it difficult to work alone, these sessions could be well worth the money. Another advantage of these types of workshops, of course, is that you get to meet other people like

yourself who want to do something to improve either their job prospects, promotion possibilities, self-image – or maybe a bit of all three.

3. *Peer support groups*: Sometimes APL centres do not offer portfolio development workshops as such. But they do provide a room for APL candidates to meet on a regular basis to work in small groups. These are called peer support groups: small groups of people helping and supporting one another through the APL process.

The APL centre you select may offer a range of other support services as well. Again, you will need to ask questions and perhaps be a bit persistent to make sure that you get what you want and need during your APL experience. But more than likely, you will find a number of very helpful people at your APL centre who will be eager to see you succeed.

Chapter 7

What Does Assessment Mean?

Once you have submitted your portfolio, your adviser will review it for completeness. He or she will check it over to make sure it is properly organized, numbered and legible. Your adviser will then arrange for your assessor(s) to receive it and begin your actual assessment. This chapter will describe what you can anticipate at this stage of your APL work.

THE ASSESSMENT PROCESS

The assessment process begins with your assessor reviewing and evaluating your portfolio. It ends with your assessor deciding whether or not you will be awarded the credit or qualification you are seeking. You may find it useful to refer to Figure 7.1 which gives you an overview of the APL assessment process. We shall look carefully at each step.

Your assessor will begin the assessment process by carefully considering the evidence you have presented against each of the requirements or standards of the qualification you are seeking. As someone who has been trained in assessment, you can expect that your assessor will be:

- an expert in the area(s) in which you have asked to be assessed;
- familiar with the standards or requirements of the qualification you are seeking;
- able to apply the basic principles of relevance, authenticity, currency and sufficiency (see Chapter 6) to your evidence; and
- committed to carrying out the assessment as fairly and professionally as possible.

Once the assessor has completed his or her initial evaluation of your portfolio, he or she will make one of two decisions: (1) the evidence you submitted *can be* accepted as conclusive proof that you have met the standards or requirements of the qualification; or (2) the evidence you submitted *cannot* stand as conclusive proof that you have met the standards or requirements of the qualification *yet*.

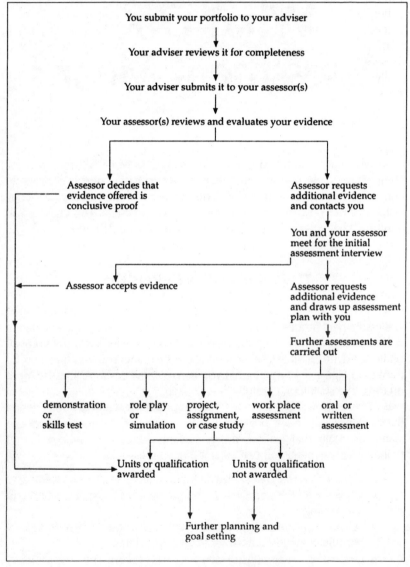

Figure 7.1 *The assessment process*

In all probability – especially if your are applying for an entire qualification or a substantial portion of one – your assessor will require *some* additional evidence or information from you. If, for example, you are seeking credit for a number of NVQ units, the assessor may be satisfied with some but seek additional evidence for others. Almost always at least some of this additional evidence will be obtained during a discussion or oral interview with you, although it can be in the form of a written request to you for more evidence, either direct or indirect.

It is important to add that if your assessor requires additional information from you, this is not a reflection on the quality of the evidence you presented. Remember that it is your assessor's job to make sure that you really can do and know what you claim. If your evidence is insufficient, this does not mean it is not of high quality. It simply means that your assessor is doing the best job he or she can.

THE INITIAL ASSESSMENT INTERVIEW

If you are required to meet your assessor, what can you expect? First of all, you will be contacted by either your assessor or your adviser so that a suitable meeting time can be arranged. At many APL centres this will be confirmed in writing. As necessary you will also be given a map and any instructions about parking or public transport.

If your assessor has asked for additional physical evidence, this too will be discussed with you on the telephone and ideally confirmed in writing. There should be sufficient time between the initial contact you have with your assessor and your actual meeting date for you to collect or develop the evidence requested.

Your assessor may also let you know in advance the particular units or sections of your portfolio he or she will be asking you about.

At the initial assessment interview, your assessor will give you feedback on the evidence you submitted in the portfolio. He or she will tell you what was acceptable and what was not. He or she will also tell you what else is needed to help him or her make the necessary decisions regarding your claims to credit.

In general the purpose of the initial assessment interview is to:

- allow the assessor to ask you specific questions about what you know and can do, based on the evidence presented in your portfolio and your claims to credit;
- allow the assessor to ask you questions about the evidence in your portfolio, most often to clarify particular pieces;
- confirm that the evidence you presented really is your work (authenticity!); and

■ negotiate with you any further assessments as may be necessary.

By the end of the interview you will have a clear idea of exactly where you stand: either you will have been recommended for accreditation or you will have agreed an assessment plan which will allow you to produce further evidence of your competence.

ASSESSMENT OPTIONS

If your assessor requires you to undertake one or more assessments, the chances are that these will fall into the following categories:

1. Demonstration or skills test.
2. Role play or simulation.
3. Project, assignment or case study.
4. Assessment in the workplace.
5. Oral or written questioning.

Each one of these types of assessment is intended to allow you to generate further evidence to support your claims to credit. You can prepare for these by thinking about what each will ask you to do.

1. *Demonstration or skills test*: this asks you to do something: you will have to demonstrate what it is you claim you *can* do. For example, if you say you know how to use a word-processor, you will be asked to create and print-out one or more documents; if you say you know how to use a lathe, again you will be asked to use it in a practical situation. You can anticipate that you will be asked to demonstrate the range of competences as spelled out in the standards or requirements of the qualification you are seeking.

Most often you will be asked to complete the demonstration or skills test in the presence of the assessor or someone else from the Centre approved by the assessor. Prior to the assessment, you will most likely be given time to familiarize yourself with the equipment you are to use or the situation in which you are to perform. If you are not given time to feel reasonably comfortable with the situation in which you are to demonstrate your skills, you can politely ask for a bit more time.

How to prepare: to prepare for a demonstration or skills test, you will want to practise as much as you can, always keeping in mind the standards or requirements you are trying to meet. However, it may be that what you will be asked to do as part of your assessment is something you do all the time in which case you may not need to practise at all, or maybe just a bit. You'll still want to make sure you are familiar with the standards or requirements so you will be sure to satisfy the assessor that you can work to the level of performance expected.

2. *Role play or simulation*: role play or simulation assessments are another type of demonstration. But unlike a skills test, you generally will be asked to perform in either an imaginary situation or one that only *reflects* the real situation in which you are likely to perform outside the assessment situation. For example, suppose that you are hoping to earn credit for your interviewing skills. Perhaps the evidence from your place of work is confidential and you are not able to secure it. In this case, your assessor may suggest one or more role plays – an imaginary situation – in which you would be asked to perform, to demonstrate your interviewing skills. In this particular example, you would be given the basic 'facts' of the situation and the assessor or someone else might play the part of the client or interviewee who you would be asked to interview. As with the skills test, the assessor would still be assessing your performance based on the standards or requirements of the qualification you were seeking.

A simulation is similar, but not quite the same. Most of us are familiar with the 'simulators' used to train airplane pilots: the simulator is an exact replica of the inside of a cockpit and the pilot is asked to perform all the necessary manoeuvres required to fly and land the plane. Another good example might be the APL candidate who is seeking a qualification in health care and has to demonstrate resuscitation. In this case, the candidate might be asked to demonstrate the correct procedures on a model of a human being. Simulations, like role plays, are generally used when it is not possible or cost effective to gain evidence from any other source.

How to prepare: again you will want to practise, as necessary, using your friends, family or colleagues. It is always best, of course, if they can present you with various challenges so you will have an opportunity to demonstrate a range of skills and knowledge. You might at first feel awkward or silly practising in this way but, in the end, a few practice runs can significantly reduce your anxiety and improve your chances for doing well during your actual assessment.

3. *Project, assignment or case study*: if your assessor gives you a project, assignment or case study to complete, you will be asked to produce something – whether a written report or something else. The project or assignment will relate to the unit for which you are seeking credit and will give you an opportunity to generate evidence that shows you can meet the standards. Sometimes you will be asked to undertake a particular project or assignment in your place of work; others may ask you to do something as part of your community work. In either case you and your assessor will need to negotiate and agree the expected outcome of your work and a specific length of time by which your work – and your assessment – will be complete.

If the assessor asks you to analyse a case study, in all likelihood this will be accompanied by a set of questions you will be expected to answer. You will be asked to use the case study to stimulate your thoughts and problem-solving skills. You may be asked to present an oral as well as a written report as an outcome of your case study analysis.

How to prepare: it is difficult to give advice on how to prepare for a project, assignment or case study because they can vary so much. You will need to be guided by your assessor and question anything that seems unclear. You also will want to be sure to have your work completed by the agreed date or, if you have a serious problem, let your assessor know as soon as possible that your work will be late.

4. *Assessment in the workplace*: more and more assessments are taking place in the workplace, that is, a supervisor or outside assessor observes someone working under normal conditions and uses the standards to make their assessments of that person. As part of your APL assessment, you may be assessed in one of two ways in the workplace:

1. In one situation, your assessor may come to your place of work, or where you are performing, to observe you. Some recent examples include assessors going to the concert hall, the local pub, the garden centre, a retail shop and a local restaurant. In each case the assessor was able to view the candidate working under the normal conditions of his or her workplace. On some occasions this type of assessment may put additional demands on you. For example, if your place of work is not generally open to the public, you will need to make sure that your supervisor and colleagues agree that it is OK for your assessor to come to your workplace. Issues of health and safety, security, production schedules and confidentiality may all be reasons why this would not be the best way for you to be assessed. You will need to work out the details and expectations of this type of workplace assessment very carefully with both your assessor and those with whom you work.

2. Another type of workplace assessment involves your supervisor or someone else in the organization assessing you. If you are completing APL through your employer, this type of assessment will no doubt be considered as a standard part of your overall assessment. If, however, your APL centre is separate from your place of work, it may be that your supervisor or someone else within the organization will need to conduct the assessment and write on your behalf (see letters of validation in Chapter 6). Sometimes, of course, your assessor and your supervisor may discuss and agree the best way to help you generate the evidence you will need.

How to prepare: the best way you can prepare for *any* workplace assessment is to do the best job you can. Again, being familiar with the standards and making sure your work reflects the best practice described by the standards is the surest way of doing well in your workplace assessment.

5. *Oral or written questioning*: this type of assessment generally asks you to respond to a set of questions. The questions usually will be geared to helping you prove what you *know*. Unlike the other types of assessment, which mostly are about performing, oral or written questioning is generally about testing your knowledge. For many qualifications, what you know is just as important as what you can do.

Oral assessments are straightforward. If you are asked to undergo this type of assessment, the assessor will let you know the material to be covered and will then develop a set of questions for you to respond to orally. He or she may need to tape-record your answers. Although this may seem a bit intimidating at first, it is most definitely for your benefit: it provides the needed proof that you answered the questions satisfactorily.

There are many different types of written assessment. These include: multiple-choice questions, short-answer questions and essays.

If you are asked to take a multiple-choice test, you will be given a series of questions and a set of possible answers for each. You will be expected to select the one you believe best answers the question.

Short-answer questions require just that: short answers. You will be given a question and asked to write in your own words the correct answer.

Essay tests, like some case study analyses, generally ask you to write more extensively on a particular topic, analysing a given problem, interpreting information, or using different types of information in a unique way.

In each case the assessor will mark or grade the test and you will be given the results.

How to prepare: the best way to prepare for an oral or written assessment is to make sure you know what is going to be covered. As part of your APL assessment, you have a right to know the general areas to be assessed, if not the specific questions. You may also find it helpful to familiarize yourself with the various types of assessment you are to be given. You may also be able to get some sample questions beforehand to practise. This is strongly recommended because if you are not familiar with different types of questions and the types of answers that are acceptable, your own answers may not reflect what you actually know and understand.

You can ask either your assessor or your adviser for help in this area. Both may be able to refer you to books that discuss various types of written assessment and in some cases you may be able to attend a workshop or seminar to help you prepare.

It is worth remembering that however difficult your assessment may seem at the time, it is *your* opportunity to prove what you know and can do.

Through the APL process you have several different chances to meet the standards or requirements. In that sense you have significant control over your assessment and indeed will find that more often than not your assessor will be happy to work *with* you – to find the most appropriate ways of allowing you to prove what you know and can do.

Whether during the initial assessment interview or on other occasions, most APL candidates find that meeting their assessor is not only helpful, it is also reassuring. Having the opportunity to talk about what you know and can do or answer questions about the evidence you have supplied can only help your case.

RECEIVING FEEDBACK

Throughout the assessment process, your assessor will be giving you feedback. Whenever possible, this will be at the time of your assessment. However, if you have had to complete a project, assignment or case study or have had to take a written assessment, there may be a delay. In light of the outcomes of your additional assessments, your assessor also may want to go back and review some of the evidence in your portfolio. In these circumstances there may be a delay in hearing the results of your assessments. However, if you have not heard anything within two or three weeks after your last assessment, you may want to contact your adviser or assessor to learn if there has been a problem.

GETTING YOUR RESULTS

Most often, you will receive the official results of your APL assessment in writing. These results will either state that:

(a) you should be awarded the credits or qualification you were seeking; or
(b) the credits or qualification cannot *yet* be awarded.

If you have been recommended for credit, your centre will complete all the necessary paper work to ensure that you receive the award you deserve. This may require an outside body – an awarding body – checking the assessment first (see Chapter 3) or if you are at a polytechnic or university, it may simply require some administrative procedures at another office.

Remember, too, that if you are seeking an NVQ or SVQ you may have earned only some of the units necessary for the full qualification. If this is the case, you will want to discuss a number of different options with your adviser to make sure you can achieve the entire qualification. Some of these options are outlined in Chapter 8.

If your assessor has not recommended you for credit at this time, he or she will have told you why. You will then have a number of choices to make regarding how you wish to proceed. Both your assessor and your adviser will be able to help you with your future decisions, and again various options for acquiring new learning are described in Chapter 8.

Many APL centres also have an appeals procedure. If you disagree with the assessor's decision and feel it was unfair or in some way based on an inadequate assessment of you, you may want to talk with your adviser about making use of this option.

OTHER RESPONSIBILITIES OF THE ASSESSOR

Thus far we have talked about the role of the assessor in evaluating your evidence and making decisions about whether or not you can be awarded the credit or qualification you are seeking. It may help you to work with your assessor if you are also aware of his or her other responsibilities.

1. Like your adviser, your assessor is also a record keeper. He or she must keep accurate records of each meeting with you and the outcomes of each assessment. Sometimes these records will be read by other people, for example, representatives of the awarding bodies. In all cases, you can ask to be shown what has been written about you. As was mentioned above, sometimes assessors also must keep tape recordings of their oral assessments. Most individuals would probably prefer not to make these recordings, but they are required to do so by many of the awarding bodies as part of ensuring good quality in assessment practice.

2. Your assessor is also an important part of the APL team at your centre. In this capacity he or she will regularly meet your adviser and provide information about both technical and non-technical issues in the APL process. For example, if, while you are gathering your evidence, you identify a problem of evidence that stumps your adviser, he or she may seek help and guidance from your assessor.

3. Your assessor may also be the liaison person with the awarding body whose qualification you are seeking. In this role, your assessor will be able to obtain information regarding the interpretation of the standards, the use of particular types of evidence and so forth. To a very large extent, the work of your assessor is dependent on the guidelines laid down by someone else or agreed by a significant number of subject specialists in the same area.

4. Lastly, your assessor may also be a lecturer, a supervisor or have some other work in addition to his or her APL assessment responsibilities. For this

reason, you may not always be able to reach him or her when you wish. (The same may be true for your adviser, for that matter.) At the very beginning of the APL process you should ask about the best times to telephone your adviser and the assessor. Most assessor and advisers maintain regular office hours. They should let you have these hours so you can plan your phone calls or visits appropriately.

QUESTIONS ABOUT THE ASSESSMENT PROCESS

Almost always APL candidates have questions about the assessment process. No doubt you have – or will! As we did in the last chapter, let us see if we can anticipate some of yours by answering some of those that are more frequently asked:

What if I am seeking accreditation in more than one area, for example in catering and business studies, will the same assessor assess both areas?
No, most often you will have a different assessor for each area in which you are seeking credit – unless one assessor happens to be an expert in both areas. Since the whole credibility of the APL process is based on subject specialists making assessment decisions, it will be important that each assessment is done properly and by a trained specialist in your area(s).

How long will the assessment process take?
There is no set length of time. Sometimes an assessment may be completed within one week; in some cases it may take several. A lot will depend on the number of units for which you are seeking credit, the number of assessors involved, the sufficiency of the evidence in your portfolio and the number of additional assessments you may be asked to complete.

How much will it cost?
Again, each centre sets its fees differently. You will want to ask about the fees right at the beginning of the APL process. You should be told in writing, and again, if anything is not clear, ask about it.

How do I deal with my anxiety?
Most people are naturally a bit nervous or anxious either before or during their assessments. This is to be expected. The best way to deal with it is to prepare as thoroughly as possible – practise to reassure yourself, ask for feedback on your performance at work or in other contexts, make sure you know and understand the standards and the type of assessment you will be asked to undergo, *and* lastly, be sure to get a good night's sleep!

What about these awarding bodies, can they override the decisions made by my assessor?
Most often awarding body representatives work closely with each APL

centre offering its qualifications. Many actively promote the use of APL (see Appendix 3) and to that end monitor the work of each APL centre carefully. Although it is rare for an awarding body to overturn the decisions made by a local centre, it is possible. In these cases, the assessor, perhaps the adviser, and the awarding body representatives will review the details of your evidence. If additional evidence or information is needed, the adviser or assessor will advise you. Although you need to know that this *could* happen, the actual number of cases is rare, so it is not something you should be actively concerned about.

No doubt you will have your own questions about the APL assessment process. You can use the worksheet shown in Figure 7.2 to write them down. You may want to ask these at your APL centre.

Figure 7.2   *Assessment questions worksheet*

We have come just about to the end of the APL process, but no doubt now you want to know what happens next. We'll go to the last chapter to find out.

Chapter 8

Making Your Success Work For You

When you receive the results of your APL assessment, you will no doubt experience a number of feelings. You may be so overjoyed that you received all the credit or the qualification you were seeking, you want to rush out and celebrate. Or maybe you will feel a bit let down because you didn't get everything you had hoped for. And of course, you may feel something in between. For each person the end of the APL process can mean something different. In almost all cases, however, it represents some sort of new beginning.

Many people who begin the APL process think it represents the end of a long journey and indeed, perhaps for some it does. But just like so many other valuable life experiences, the end of the APL process often represents the start of a new journey. It helps people to make new decisions about themselves and what they want to do next.

Regardless of the outcomes of your assessment, you probably have learned a lot about yourself. You may want to go back and think about your original goal or maybe you want to set some new targets for yourself. Clearly by knowing more about yourself, you will be in a stronger position to make new decisions about yourself. In this chapter you will review some of the options you have for making the most of the success you achieve through APL.

SETTING NEW GOALS

Depending on the outcomes of your APL assessment, you may have an immediate goal – to finish what you set out to achieve. For example, you may have been accredited for some of the units in an NVQ or SVQ but not all; or perhaps you received an entire qualification but view this achievement as a stepping stone to the one you really would like or need; or again, perhaps because of your APL experience, you simply want to develop yourself in a new area. In any event you may need to acquire new skills and knowledge. You will want to decide which are the best ways to get what you need.

NEW LEARNING

Today, more than ever, adults have literally dozens of options by which they can acquire the skills and knowledge they need. Never before have there been so many new learning options to choose from. No doubt in your discussions with your adviser, some of these may already have been described to you, but if you are reading this book without the benefit of an adviser, it is worth making a note of some of the more popular routes.

Flexible workshops and/or short courses
Your own APL centre may offer a range of workshops or short courses to help you 'top-up' your skills and knowledge. Sometimes you can make use of traditional courses as well on a 'drop-in' basis. If you need 'just a little bit' to complete the qualification you've been aiming for, you may want to explore this possibility with your adviser.

Distance or open learning
Distance or open learning options mean that you can learn where and when you want. You are not restricted by a particular time and place for a course. Rather, you receive instruction at a distance from the college or training organization providing the course or instruction. The college or training organization will mail you books, worksheets, audio cassettes or other materials which you can use in your home or place of work. You complete assignments on a regular basis, mail them to your tutor or mentor and in return receive the next lesson or sets of materials. In most programmes you also have an opportunity to speak with a tutor or mentor on a regular basis. Your adviser may have information about many different kinds of open and distance learning programmes. Two of the better known ones, however, are the Open College and the Open University. Their addresses are provided at the end of Appendix 3.

In addition to these traditional methods of open and distance learning, there are a number of other flexible options you may want to learn more about. These include television and radio instruction, satellite transmissions, and computer networks, to name but a few. Again, your adviser may be able to help you identify sources of information or you may want to contact your local library or Training and Enterprise Council (TEC). Most TECs have

Information and Advice Units which will have information on many of the courses or training options available in your area.

Work-based learning
Work-based learning is yet another way to obtain the skills and knowledge you need. Employers all over Britain are increasingly providing new opportunities for their employees to learn in the workplace, whether on-the-job or through special, off-the-job training programmes. Many are also committed to taking on students enrolled in a college or university and providing 'work placement' opportunities.

Learning in the workplace is an ideal way to achieve vocational qualifications, in particular NVQs and SVQs which are based on performance in the workplace. But it can also be a very useful addition to the learning that takes place in the classroom whether for vocational or academic qualifications.

For example, you may want to explore with your APL centre *and* your employer (if you are in work) the possibility of creating new opportunities for you to learn in the workplace. Many colleges and companies are working cooperatively to help larger numbers of people make good use of *all* the learning opportunities that exist in both contexts. And indeed many companies are actively participating in programmes such as 'Investors in People'.[1] These programmes are designed to promote more and better learning in the workplace. If you can, you will want to make good use of as many of these opportunities as possible.

Learning contracts
A learning contract spells out a learning programme that will lead towards a specified and desired outcome for an individual. It is usually entered into by individuals, their employers and an education partner. A learning contract lets you spell out how you want to achieve certain learning objectives. By setting particular goals or targets, each partner entering into the learning contract has a clear idea of his or her responsibilities and the likely outcomes. Again, if your APL centre (or your employer) offers you the opportunity of entering into a learning contract, you may want to explore how it could benefit you in meeting the requirements or standards of the qualification you are hoping to achieve.

It is perhaps worth noting that sometimes APL is actually a part of a learning contract. A learning contract is another way of setting a target for yourself. If it includes APL, your learning contract will allow you to say, for example, 'This is what I am going to try to *earn* through APL; this is how I am

[1] 'Investors in People' is a new National Standard which has been launched to help British business get the most out of its people. It is based on the practical experience of businesses that have improved their performance through investing in people.

going to *learn* what I need to learn, and this is what I *expect* to happen in work and in the classroom so I can reach my learning targets.'

Each of these options has something different to offer you. And of course, you don't want to exclude the possibility of traditional courses either. Sometimes they can provide the best alternative to help you gain the skills and knowledge you need. Remember, too, that many college, polytechnics and universities offer courses in the evening as well as during the day.

CAREER PLANNING

In addition to needing to acquire new skills and knowledge, you may also want to change your job. As we highlighted in Chapter 1, you may want to enter the job market for the first time, re-enter after an extended or short absence, seek a promotion, or change direction altogether. If you have earned the qualification you set out to acquire, you need now to make it work for you.

If you are very clear about the job or career you want, you are probably a lot closer to getting it than you think! At least you know what you are looking for. For so many people, finding a new or better job is a double burden, because while they know they are dissatisfied with their current situation, they have no real sense of where they want to go or how to get there. But there are a number of possibilities for obtaining help.

1. Your APL centre may offer a careers service which could help you clarify the type of work you would like to do and provide you with information about the availability of jobs in your area.
2. Similarly, your local TEC may also offer advice and guidance to help you. The TEC may have a number of computer data bases to give you up-to-date job and career information.
3. Your local library or the one at your APL centre may carry a whole range of books, magazines and leaflets on finding a job or beginning a new career.
4. A number of private and government-sponsored career advice services are also available. You may want to check in your Yellow Pages under 'Careers Advice' to learn the names, addresses and phone numbers of advisers nearest to you.
5. There may also be a number of self-help groups in your areas sponsored by one or more community groups.

Armed with the new qualification you have achieved, it should be much easier for you to identify and secure the job you want. On the other hand, finding a new job is never easy. You have to be persistent, spend time at it, be willing to ask a lot of questions, and be assessed, either formally or informally. In other words, the same skills you used to earn yourself credit through APL could help you in your job search too!

THE NEW YOU

Acquiring new learning or a new job are just two of the ways you can build on the success of your APL experience. There are many others. Many people who complete the process are surprised at how many other things change for them too. They find it easier to make new friends, pursue new interests, ask questions, assert themselves in new situations and otherwise feel more self-confident and pleased with themselves. Here are some statements made by some recent APL candidates:

- 'I was so surprised that I could be successful at something. Until APL I didn't have a lot of success in my life . . .'
- 'Now I know I can set a goal for myself and go for it . . .'
- 'My adviser and assessor were so helpful, I've developed a new respect for academics and what they have to offer . . .'
- 'I didn't realize that there were so many others like me – people who felt like they were failures because they didn't have a particular qualification . . .'
- 'I still can't believe that I earned an entire qualification in three months! Now I feel like anything is possible.'
- 'Until I got this qualification, my family thought I was pretty useless . . .'
- 'I learned so much about myself in the process, I feel like a new person . . .'

This is how some people have benefited from their APL experiences. You might want to take a minute to think about how you have changed as a result of your APL work too. Do you have a different sense of yourself and all you know and can do? Do you think about other people in any new ways? Do you have a greater sense of control in your life? Do you feel more able to take on new challenges? You may be surprised at the range of answers you come up with.

As you reflect on your own experience, let us return to some of the people we introduced in Chapter 1 and see how – if – APL led them to the goals they were seeking.

Case Studies

Clair M. was able to earn an NVQ Level 2 in Business Administration (Office Procedures) offered by the RSA Examinations Board. From this she was able to get an interview with the firm that had originally expressed interest in her and eventually secure a full-time job. Clair hopes now to go on to achieve a second qualification in Business Administration (Secretarial Procedures) Level 3 and is trying to keep her 'evidence' up to date. She has learned now how to use the standards and apply them to her work – so much so that a number of other people within the company are also thinking about getting NVQs.

Erik S. is now enrolled in a degree programme at a polytechnic. Through APL he was able to get advanced standing and is now working to complete all the necessary requirements to earn his degree. Because of Erik's knowledge and experience with computers, his lecturers regularly call on him to give examples of computer applications in the workplace. In addition, many of the traditional-aged students also find Erik a valuable resource, especially around exam time!

Sally B. has been accredited for several units towards *two* NVQs – one in Health Care (Assisting Clients in Care), Level 1; and Social Care (Residential, Domiciliary and Day Care), Level 2. Her adviser has helped her to see the value of all she has done and is encouraging her to obtain other units, now in the area of business administration. Sally isn't sure at this point whether she wants an entire qualification. She says she will decide after she's done some 'stacking up' of units. She has joined a 'peer support group' through her APL centre and looks forward to its monthly meetings.

Brian A. is enrolled on a management development course at a leading management development centre. He hopes to receive a BTEC certifcate in management and has already earned five units towards the qualification through his APL work. He is making use of the distance learning opportunities the centre offers and at the suggestion of his assessor is using his own work situation to generate evidence for some of the other units in the qualification. For Brian, using the standards in conjunction with the learning materials provided by the centre has led him to learn a lot about the way he could be doing things better. Both he and his boss are pleased with not just his skills but his ability to work more effectively to solve the personnel problems that were so continuously weighing him down.

Gita W. is working towards a SCOTVEC qualification in business administration. She has been able to earn credit for modules in financial recording, cash handling, starting a small business and a few others. But this has not been an easy time for her. Because of her estrangement from her parents she has had little or no evidence from her 'prior achievements'. For almost every module she has had to undergo either a demonstration or complete an assignment. But as she says, 'It's still saving me valuable time and I'm learning a lot in the process.'

Bill W. went to his APL centre hoping to be told which qualification to seek. Not only did his adviser not tell him which qualification to try for, she suggested that he enrol on a 'returning to learning' workshop that the college was offering. The adviser helped Bill to see that (a) he was good at many things and (b) that in the long run he would be better off choosing a new job that would allow him to use many of the skills and abilities that he had but was not able to apply in his current job. The adviser also helped him to see that a little boost to his self-confidence wouldn't be bad either. Bill has put APL on hold until he decides what he really wants to do.

So these are the stories of six people who thought APL had something to offer and who were determined to make their APL success work for them. What about you, are you ready to make yours work for you?

Appendix 1

Background to the New Qualifications

The idea of having NVQs and SVQs evolved during the 1980s when it became clear to government policy-makers, employers, national organizations such as the Confederation of British Industry and the Trades Union Congress, and many others, that the British vocational education and training system was unable to meet the very great demand for a highly skilled and flexible work force.

Gradually over the decade a number of good ideas were put forward:

- that if there were clear standards about what people should be able to do in the workplace, each person would have something to work towards;
- that if more people had qualifications based on these standards, employers and the individuals themselves would have a better idea of the skills and knowledge they actually possessed;
- that these occupational standards might best be determined by people who actually did the work, not only by educators and trainers;
- that a national organization should be set up to oversee the development of the new qualifications which were to be based on these standards.

As a result of these and other ideas, a number of important activities were undertaken.

- The National Council for Vocational Qualifications was established. This is the organization that monitors and ensures the quality of the new qualifications.
- The Employment Department provided money for industry representatives to come together to develop the new occupational standards. These industry representatives form groups called Industry Lead Bodies (ILB). Once an ILB has developed the standards that it thinks best represents its industry, it develops qualifications based on those standards. The NCVQ puts its stamp of approval on these new qualifications if the qualifications meet NCVQs own standards of quality.
- People working to obtain these qualifications all have access to the

standards, so that they and their employers, teachers and trainers all know what they are working towards.

- NCVQ does not award these qualifications. They are awarded by many of the traditional awarding bodies and by some of the Industry Lead Bodies who have also become partners in awarding qualifications.

Appendix 2

National Vocational Qualifications by Area of Competence

Entries marked * have passed their expiry date but are within certification end period.

1 TENDING ANIMALS, PLANTS AND LAND

1.1 – **Agriculture (Foundation)** Level 1, NPTC, NEBAHAI;[1] **Agriculture (Beef Production)** Level 2; **Agriculture (Dairy Production)** Level 2; **Agriculture (General Livestock Production)** Level 2; **Agriculture (General Mechanized Crop Production)** Level 2; **Agriculture (Goat Production)** Level 2; **Agriculture (Hatchery Production)** Level 2; **Agriculture (Pig Production)** Level 2; **Agriculture (Poultry Production)** Level 1; **Agriculture (Poultry Production)** Level 2; **Agriculture (Sheep Production)** Level 2; **Gamekeeping** Level 2, *plus* JCFHG.

1.2 – **Commercial Horticulture (Crop Production)** Level 1; **Commercial Horticulture (Mushroom Production)** Level 1; **Commercial Horticulture (Fruit Production)** Level 2; **Commercial Horticulture (Mushroom Production)** Level 2; **Commercial Horticulture (Protected Cropping)** Level 2; **Commercial Horticulture (Outdoor Vegetable Production)** Level 2; **Commercial Horticulture (Nursery Stock Produc-**

---

[1] See Appendix 3 for the meaning of initials. All entries under 1.1 and 1.2 are administered by NPTC and NEBAHAI. Where other initials are shown, the Body or Bodies are *in addition to* NPTC and NEBAHAI.

tion) Level 2; **Commercial Horticulture (Garden Centre Operations)** Level 1; **Commercial Horticulture (Garden Centre Operations)** Level 2; **Forestry (Foundation)** Level 1, *plus* FTC; **Forestry** Level 2, *plus* FTC.

1.3 – **Guide Dogs (Kennel Staff)** Level 2, C&G;[1] **Guide Dogs (Trainer)** Level 2; **Kennel Supervision** Level 3.

1.4 – **Sea Fishing** Level 1, *plus* SFIA; **Sea Fishing** Level 2, *plus* SFIA.

2   EXTRACTING AND PROVIDING NATURAL RESOURCES

2.2 – **Operating Dump-Trucks** Level 1, CCBCITB;[2] **Operating Bulldozers/ Traxcavators** Level 2; **Operating Excavators** Level 2.

2.3 – **Water Distribution (Service Laying)** Level 2, CABWI;[3] **Water Distribution (Mains Laying)** Level 2.

2.4 – **Iron and Steel Production (Foundation)** Level 1, C&G, SILB.

3   CONSTRUCTING

3.2 – **Constructing (Bricklaying)** Level 2, CITB, C&G, CITB(NI), JCBCENI;[4] **Construction (Bricklaying)** Level 3; **Construction (Bench Joinery)** Level 2; **Construction (Carpentry and Joinery)** Level 2; **Construction (Carpentry and Joinery)** Level 3; **Construction (Demountable Partitioning)** Level 2, *not* C&G; **Construction (Wood Machining)** Level 3; **Construction (Built-up Felt Roofing)** Level 3, *plus* NJCFRCI; **Construction (Roof Slating and Tiling)** Level 3; **Constructing (Roof Sheeting and Cladding)** Level 3, *plus* NFRC; **Construction (Mastic Asphalting)** Level 3, *plus* NJCMAI; **Construction (General Building Operations)** Level 2; **Construction (Plant Maintenance Mechanics)** Level 2, *plus* CECCB; **Construction (Basic Scaffolding)** Level 2, *not* C&G; **Construction (Advanced Scaffolding)** Level 3, *not* C&G; **Construction (Contractors Plant Mechanics)** Level 3, *plus* CECCB; **Construction (Stonemasonry)** Level 3; **Construction (Painting and Decorating)** Level 2; **Construction (Painting and Decorating)** Level 3; **Construction (Plastering)** Level 2; **Construction (Plastering)** Level 3; **Construction (Floorlaying)** Level 3, *plus* CFA; **Construction (Wall and Floor Tiling)** Level 3; **Construction (Glazing)** Level 3, *plus* NJCFGI; **Construction (Fencing)** Level 2; **Construction (Ceiling Fixing)** Level 2.

3.3 – **Construction (Shop Fitting)** Level 3

3.4 – **Electrical Installations (Construction)** Level 3, JIBECI, C&G; **Installing and**

---

[1] All entries under 1.3 and 1.4 are administered by C&G (see Appendix 3).
[2] All entries under 2.2 are administered by CCBCITB.
[3] Both entries under 2.3 are administered by CABWI.
[4] All entries under 3.2 and 3.3 are administered by these Bodies, with additions or exceptions as stated.

Commissioning Telecommunications Terminal Equipment (Radio) Level 2, TVSC; Installing and Commissioning Telecommunications Terminal Equipment (Fixed) Level 2, TVSC; Installing and Testing Telecommunications Switching and Transmission Equipment Level 2, TVSC; Heating and Ventilating (Fitting and Welding) Level 3, CITB, C&G, CITB(NI), JCBCENI, HVDENJC.

4 ENGINEERING

4.3 – Maintaining PSVs (Body Trades) Level 1, BCTL;[1] Maintaining PSVs (Electrical) Level 1; Maintaining PSVs (Mechanical) Level 1; Automotive Glazing Level 2, GTL, RTITB only; Maintaining PSVs (Body Trades) Level 2; Maintaining PSVs (Electrical) Level 2; Maintaining PSVs (Mechanical) Level 2; Maintaining PSVs (Body Trades) Level 3; Maintaining PSVs (Electrical) Level 3; Maintaining PSVs (Mechanical) Level 3.

4.4 – Operating and Controlling Power Station Systems: Fossil Fired (Electricity Generation) Level 1, ETA, BTEC;[2] Operating and Controlling Power Station Boilers (Electricity Generation) Level 2; Operating Power Station Systems: Coal, Dust and Ash (Electricity Generation) Level 2; Operating and Controlling Power Station Units: Fossil Fired (Electricity Generation) Level 2; Operating and Controlling Power Station Turbines (Electricity Generation) Level 2; Operating and Controlling Power Station Systems: Fossil Fired (Electricity Generation) Level 3; Overhead Lines and Equipment: Installation and Maintenance (Electricity Transmission and Generation) Level 3*, plus C&G; Metering Equipment: Installation and Maintenance (Electricity Distribution) Level 3*, plus C&G; Telecommunications Equipment: Installation and Maintenance (Electricity Transmission and Distribution) Level 3*, plus C&G; Thermal Material and Associated Equipment: Removal, Preparing and Fixing (Electricity Generation) Level 3*, plus C&G; Wiring Systems and Appliances: Installation and Maintenance (Electricity Distribution) Level 3*, plus C&G; Control and Instrumentation Equipment: Installation and Maintenance (Electricity Generation) Level 3*, not BTEC but plus C&G; Electrical Plant and Equipment: Installation and Maintenance (Electricity Generation) Level 3*, not BTEC but plus C&G; Substation Plant and Equipment: Installation and Maintenance (Electricity Transmission and Distribution) Level 3*, plus C&G; Cables and Joints: Installation and Maintenance (Electricity Distribution) Level 3*, not BTEC but plus C&G; Mechanical Plant and Equipment: Installation and Maintenance (Electricity Generation, Transmission and Distribution) Level 3*, not BTEC but plus C&G; Electronic Office Systems Maintenance Level 1, C&G only; Electronic Office Systems Maintenance (Workshop) Level 2, C&G only; Electronic Office Systems Maintenance (Field) Level 2, C&G only.

4.5 – Shipbuilding and Marine Engineering (Foundation) Level 1, M&ETA;[3] Shipbuilding and Marine Engineering Technician (Foundation) Level 1; Shipbuild-

---

[1] All entries under 4.3 are administered by BCTL unless otherwise stated.
[2] All entries under 4.4 are administered by ETA and BTEC, with additions or exceptions as stated.
[3] All entries under 4.5 are administered by M&ETA.

ing and Marine Engineering (Services) Level 2; **Shipbuilding and Marine Engineer-
ing (Structures)** Level 2; **Shipbuilding and Marine Engineering (Outfitting)** Level 2;
Shipbuilding and Marine Engineering Technician Level 3; **Shipbuilding and Marine
Engineering** Level 3; **Shipbuilding and Marine Engineering Supervision (Technical)**
Level 3; **Shipbuilding and Marine Engineering Supervision (Skills)** Level 3;
Shipbuilding and Marine Engineering Management Level 4; **Shipbuilding and
Marine Engineering Technician Engineer** Level 4; **Joining Metal Plate by Manual
Metal Arc and Semi Automatic Critical Process** Level 3; **Joining Metal Pipe by
Manual Metal Arc and Semi-Automatic Critical Process** Level 3; **Joining Metal Plate
by Manual Arc and Automatic Critical Process** Level 3; **Joining Metal by Manual
Metal Arc Process to Non-Critical Standard** Level 2; **Joining Metal by Machine
Process to Non-Critical Standard** Level 2; **Joining Metal by Brazing and Oxygas
Weld Process** Level 2; **Joining Metal Plate by Manual Metal Arc Process (Tack)**
Level 1.

4.7 – **Engineering (Foundation)** Level 1*, ETCNI, C&G, BTEC;[1] **Engineering
Foundation (Man-made Fibres)** Level 1*, *not* ETCNI but *plus* MMFITAB, EnTra;
Engineering Foundation (Glass Manufacture) Level 1*, *not* ETCNI but *plus* GTL,
EnTra; **Engineering Manufacture (Foundation)** Level 2, *not* C&G, BTEC but *plus*
EnTra; **Engineering Manufacture (Craft Competences) Maintenance Practices**
Level 3, *plus* EnTra; **Engineering Manufacture (Craft Competences) Mechanical
(Fitting)** Level 3, *plus* EnTra; **Engineering Manufacture (Craft Competences)
Mechanical (Machining)** Level 3, *plus* EnTra; **Engineering Manufacture (Craft
Competences) Vehicle Body Practices** Level 3, *plus* EnTra; **Engineering Manufac-
ture (Craft Competences) Welding & Fabrication** Level 3, *plus* EnTra; **Engineering
Manufacture (Craft Competences) Electrical & Electronic** Level 3, *plus* EnTra;
**Engineering Manufacture (Craft Competences) Patternmaking, Mould Making
and Modelling** Level 3, *plus* EnTra; **Engineering Manufacture (Craft Competences)
Foundry Practices** Level 3, *plus* EnTra; **Engineering Construction** Level 3*, *plus*
EnTra; **Engineering Manufacture (Technician Competences)** Level 3, *not* C&G, but
plus EnTra; **Engineering Manufacture (Technician Engineer)** Level 4, *not* C&G, but
plus EnTra; **Engineering Maintenance (Petroleum Products Manufacture)** Level 3,
not ETCNI, but *plus* PTF, EnTra; **Engineering Maintenance (Refractories, Clay Pipes
and Allied Products Manufacture)** Level 3, *not* ETCNI but *plus* RCPAITC, EnTra;
Engineering Maintenance (Man-made Fibres Manufacture) Level 3, *not* ETCNI but
plus MMFITAB, EnTra; **Engineering Maintenance (Chemical Manufacture)** Level 3,
not ETCNI, BTEC but *plus* CIA; **Engineering Maintenance (China Clay and Ball Clay
Processing)** Level 3, *not* ETCNI but *plus* CCBCITB, EnTra; **Engineering Maintenance
(Plastics Processing)** Level 3, *not* ETCNI but *plus* BPTA, EnTra; **Engineering
Maintenance (Glass Manufacture)** Level 3, *not* ETCNI but *plus* GTL, EnTra;
**Engineering Maintenance (Biscuit, Cake, Chocolate and Confectionery Products
Manufacture)** Level 3, *not* ETCNI, C&G, but *plus* BCCCA, EnTra; **Engineering
Maintenance (Tobacco Products Manufacture)** Level 3, *not* ETCNI but *plus* TITO,
EnTra.

[1] All entries under 4.7 are administered by these Bodies, with the additions and exceptions stated.

5   MANUFACTURING

5.1 – **Glass and Glazing** Level 1, GTL;[1] **Glass Manufacturing (Handmade Domestic Glassware)** Level 1; **Scientific Glassblowing (Foundation)** Level 1; **Glass and Glazing Installation (Glazing)** Level 2; **Glass Manufacturing (Glass Container Forming)** Level 2; **Scientific Glassblowing** Level 2; **Glass and Glazing Production (Cast in Place Lamination)** Level 2; **Glass and Glazing Production (Glass Cutting)** Level 2; **Glass and Glazing Production (Glass Processing)** Level 2; **Glass and Glazing Production (Replacement Fabrications)** Level 2; **Refractories and Clay Pipes Process Operations** Level 1, RCPAITC *only*.

5.2 – **Tobacco Processing (Filter Rod Making)** Level 2, TITO, C&G;[2] **Tobacco Processing (Cigarette Packing)** Level 2; **Tobacco Processing (Cigarette Making)** Level 2; **Tobacco Processing (Loose Tobacco)** Level 2.

5.3 – **Machining (Lockstitch)** Level 1*, QFI;[3] **Machining (Overlock)** Level 1*; **Machining (General Sewing)** Level 1*; **Production Machine Sewing** Level 2; **Product Assembly (Sewing)** Level 2, NTTG *only*.

5.4 – **Meat Industry General Assistant** Level 1*, IMEAT; **Abattoir Process Operations** Level 2*, IMEAT; **Manufacturing Meat Products** Level 2*, IMEAT; **Catering Butchery Operations** Level 2*, IMEAT; **Meat Processing (Retailing)** Level 2, IOM;[4] **Meat Processing (Catering Butchery)** Level 2; **Meat Processing (Wholesaling)** Level 2; **Meat Processing (Abattoir Process Operations)** Level 2; **Meat Processing (Poultry Industry Operations)** Level 2; **Meat Processing (Manufacturing Operations)** Level 2; **Meat Processing (Manufacturing Packaging)** Level 2; **Meat Processing (Manufacturing Butchery)** Level 2.

5.6 – **Process Operations (Chemical Manufacture)** Level 1, C&G,[5] CIA; **Process Operations (Chemical Manufacture)** Level 2, CIA; **Process Operations (Chemical Manufacture)** Level 3, CIA; **Process Operations (Man-made Fibres and Film)** Level 1, MMFITAB; **Process Operations (Man-made Fibres and Film)** Level 2, MMFITAB; **Pharmaceutical Processing** Level 2, ABPI; **Pharmaceutical Processing** Level 3, ABPI; **Pharmaceutical Packaging** Level 1, ABPI; **Pharmaceutical Packaging** Level 2, ABPI.

5.7 – **Plastics Processing Operations (Extrusion Sheet)** Level 1, BPTA;[6] **Plastics Processing Operations (Extrusion Pipe/Profile)** Level 1; **Plastics Processing Operations (Blown Film)** Level 1; **Plastics Processing Operations (Injection Moulding)** Level 1; **Plastics Processing Operations (Blow Moulding)** Level 1; **Plastics Processing Operations (Compression Moulding)** Level 1; **Plastics Processing Operations (Polymer Compounding)** Level 1; **Plastics Processing Operations (Thermoforming)** Level 1; **Plastics Processing Operations (Continuous Substrate Coating)** Level 1; **Plastics Processing Operations (Extrusion Sheet)** Level 2; **Plastics Processing Operations (Extrusion Pipe/Profile)** Level 2; **Plastics Processing Operations (Blown**

---

[1] All entries under 5.1 are administered by GTL unless otherwise stated.
[2] All entries under 5.2 are administered by these Bodies.
[3] All entries under 5.3 are administered by QFI unless otherwise stated.
[4] The remaining entries under 5.4 are administered by IOM.
[5] All the entries under 5.6 are administered by C&G, with the additions listed.
[6] All entries under 5.7 are administered by BPTA.

Film) Level 2; **Plastics Processing Operations (Injection Moulding)** Level 2; **Plastics Processing Operations (Blow Moulding)** Level 2; **Plastics Processing Operations (Compression Moulding)** Level 2; **Plastics Processing Operations (Polymer Compounding)** Level 2; **Plastics Processing Operations (Thermoforming)** Level 2; **Plastics Processing Operations (Continuous Substrate Coating)** Level 2; **Thermoplastic Extrusion Setting** Level 3*; **Thermoplastic Blown Film Setting** Level 3*; **Thermoplastic Injection Moulding Setting** Level 3*; **Thermoplastic Blow Moulding Setting** Level 3*.

6 TRANSPORTING

6.1 – **Bus and Coach Driving and Customer Care** Level 2, BCTL; **Young Driver Scheme** Level 2, NJTC, RSA, RTITB; **Heavy Goods Vehicle Driving Assessment** Level 3, RTITB; **PSV Driving Instruction** Level 3, BCTL, C&G; **Heavy Goods Vehicle Driving Instruction** Level 3, RTITB.

7 PROVIDING GOODS AND SERVICES

7.2 – **Warehousing and Wholesaling** Level 1, BMF, IBM, NWTC, C&G, RSA;[1] **Warehousing and Wholesaling** Level 2.

7.3 – **Retailing** Level 1, NRTC, C&G, PEI, LCCI, RSA;[2] **Retailing** Level 2; **Retailing** Level 3, NRTC, C&G only; **Retailing** Level 4, NRTC, C&G only; **Retailing (DIY)** Level 1, not RSA; **Retailing (DIY)** Level 2, not RSA; **Retailing (Wines and Spirits)** Level 1, not RSA; **Retailing (Wines and Spirits)** Level 2, not RSA; **Retailing (Pharmacy – General)** Level 2, not RSA; **Retailing (Pharmacy – Medicines)** Level 2, not RSA; **Retailing (Agricultural Supplies)** Level 1, not RSA; **Retailing (Agricultural Supplies)** Level 2, not RSA; **Retailing (Records, Tapes, Compact Discs and Associated Products)** Level 2, not RSA; **Retailing (Confectionery, Tobacco and Newspapers)** Level 1, not RSA; **Retailing (Confectionery, Tobacco and Newspapers)** Level 2, not RSA; **Retailing (Delicatessen)** Level 2, not RSA; **Retailing (Fish)** Level 2, not RSA; **Retailing (Fresh Produce)** Level 2, not RSA; **Retailing (Meat)** Level 2, not RSA; **Meat Retailing** Level 2, IMEAT only; **Floristry** Level 1, NEBAHAI only; **Floristry** Level 2, NEBAHAI only; **Floristry** Level 3, NEBAHAI only; **Certificate in Travel Skills** Level 2, ABTANTB, C&G only; **Diploma in Travel Skills** Level 3, ABTANTB, C&G only; **Diploma in Advanced Travel Skills** Level 4, ABTANTB, C&G only; **Retailing (Furnishing)** Level 1, not RSA; **Retailing (Furnishing)** Level 2, not RSA; **Retailing (Electrical)** Level 2, not RSA; **Retailing (Hardware)** Level 1, not RSA; **Retailing (Hardware)** Level 2, not RSA; **Retailing (Jewellery)** Level 1, not RSA; **Retailing (Jewellery)** Level 2, not RSA; **Retailing (Office Systems & Stationery)** Level 1, not

---

[1] Both entries under 7.2 are administered by these Bodies.
[2] All entries under 7.3 are administered by these Bodies except where otherwise stated.

RSA; **Retailing (Office Systems & Stationery)** Level 2, *not* RSA; **Retailing (Drapery & Fashion)** Level 1, *not* RSA; **Retailing (Drapery & Fashion)** Level 2, *not* RSA.

7.4 – **Call Order Cookery** Level 1, HCTC,[1] C&G; **Hotel and Catering (Catering)** Level 1, BTEC; **General Kitchen Work** Level 1, C&G; **Baking (Bread Making) and (Flour Confectionery)** Level 2*, C&G *only*; **Hotel and Catering (Catering)** Level 2, BTEC; **Hotel and Catering (Food Preparation)** Level 2, BTEC; **Food Preparation and Cooking** Level 2, C&G; **Food Preparation and Cooking** Level 3, C&G; **Hotel, Catering and Institutional Operations (Food Preparation)** Level 3*, BTEC; **Hotel, Catering and Institutional Operations (General)** Level 3*, BTEC; **Counter Service** Level 1, C&G; **Food Service** Level 1, C&G; **Food Service** Level 3, C&G; **Hotel and Catering (Food and Drink Service)** Level 2*, BTEC; **Hotel Catering and Institutional Operations (Food and Drink Service)** Level 3, BTEC; **Licensed Trade Catering** Level 1, C&G; **Bar Service and Cellar Work** Level 1, C&G; **Food and Beverage Service** Level 2, C&G; **Hotel and Catering (Hotel Reception)** Level 1, BTEC; **Hotel, Catering and Institutional Operations (Reception)** Level 3*, BTEC; **Hospitality Management** Level 4*, BTEC; **Hotel, Catering and Institutional Management** Level 4*, BTEC; **Accommodation Service** Level 1, C&G; **Hotel and Catering (Accommodation)** Level 1, BTEC; **Hotel and Catering (Reception and Accommodation)** Level 2, BTEC; **Hotel and Catering (Hotel Reception)** Level 2, BTEC; **Hotel and Catering (Accommodation)** Level 2, BTEC; **Hotel, Catering and Institutional Operations (Accommodation)** Level 3*, BTEC.

7.7 – **Hairdressing (Afro-type Hair)** Level 2, HTB, C&G;[2] **Hairdressing** Level 2.

8 PROVIDING HEALTH, SOCIAL CARE AND PROTECTIVE SERVICES

8.1 – **Health Care (Assisting Clients in Care)** Level 1, JAB;[3] **Health Care (Enablement Care)** Level 2; **Health Care (Direct Personal Care)** Level 2.

8.2 – **Social Care (Residential, Domiciliary and Day Care)** Level 2; **Social Care (Residential, Domiciliary and Day Care)** Level 3.

8.5 – **Foundation Skills (Army)** Level 1, MOD, C&G; **Electronic Communications Operations** Level 2, C&G *only*; **Electronic Communications Operations** Level 3, C&G *only*.

---

[1] All entries under 7.4 (except **Baking**) are administered by HCTC, with either C&G or BTEC as stated.
[2] Both entries under 7.7 are administered by these Bodies.
[3] All entries aunder 8.1 and 8.2 are administered by JAB.

9   PROVIDING BUSINESS SERVICES

9.1 – **Business Administration (Foundation)** Level 1, C&G, LCCI, PEI, RSA, BTEC;[1] **Business Administration (Secretarial)** Level 2; **Business Administration (Financial)** Level 2; **Business Administration (Administrative)** Level 2; **Administration** Level 3, *not* C&G.

9.2 – **Financial Services (Building Societies)** Level 2, CBSI, RSA; **Financial Services (Pensions Administration)** Level 4, PMI.

9.3 – **Accounting** Level 4, AAT.

9.5 – **Business Administration (Information Processing)** Level 1*, RSA; **Business Administration (Information Processing)** Level 2*, RSA; **Software Systems Development** Level 4, COSIT; **Software Systems Design** Level 4, COSIT.

* Qualification has passed its expiry date but is within certification end period.

[1] All entries under 9.1 are administered by these bodies, with the exception stated.

Appendix 3

Lead Bodies, Awarding Bodies and Professional Bodies and Associations

*	Official APL policy in place.
**	Plan to develop APL policy.
No stars	Information unavailable or no formal policy stated.

Association of Accounting Technicians: 154 Clerkenwell Rd, LONDON EC1R 5AD

Association of Average Adjusters: Irongate House, Dukes Place, LONDON EC3A 7LP

Association of British Dental Surgery Assistants: 29 London St, Fleetwood, LANDS FY7 6JY

Association of the British Pharmaceutical Industry:** 12 Whitehall, LONDON SW1A 2DY

Association of British Travel Agents National Training Board:** Waterloo House, 11–17 Chertsey Rd, Woking, SURREY GY21 5AL

Association of Business Executives: 14 Worple Rd, LONDON SW19 4DD

Association of Corporate Treasurers: 12 Devereax Court, LONDON WC2R 3JJ

Association of Cost & Executive Accountants:* 141 Fonthill Rd, LONDON N4 3HF

Association of Health Care Information & Medical Records Officers: c/o Trevor Tyrrell Associates, Aunberry Arch, Aunberry Gap, Loughborough, LEICS LE11 1AA

Association of International Accountants Ltd: 2-10 St Johns St, BEDFORD MK42 0DN

Association of Legal Secretaries: The Mill, Clymping, Littlehampton, W. SUSSEX BN17 5RN

Biscuit, Cake, Chocolate and Confectionery Alliance:** 11 Green St, LONDON W1Y 3RF

British Horse Society: British Equestrian Centre, Stoneleigh, WARWICKSHIRE CV8 2LR

British Polymer Training Association: Coppice House, Halesfield 7 Telford, SHROPSHIRE TF7 4NA

British Society of Scientific Glassblowers: 21 Grebe Ave., Eccleston Park, St Helens, MERSEYSIDE WA10 3QL

Builders Merchants Federation Education & Training Department:* 5 Parnall Rd, Staple Tyre, Harlow, ESSEX CM18 7PP

Building and Allied Trades Joint Industrial Council: 14-15 Great James St, LONDON WC1N 3DP

Bus and Coach Training Limited:* Gable House, 40 High St, Rickmansworth, HERTS WD3 1ER

Business and Technician Education Council:* Central House, Upper Woburn Place, LONDON WC1H 0HH

Central Council for Education and Training in Social Work: Derbyshire House, St Chad's House, St Chad's St, LONDON WC1H 8AD

Certification and Assessment Board for The Water Industry: Water Services Association, 1 Queen Anne's Gate, LONDON SW1H 9BT

Chartered Association of Certified Accountants: 29 Lincoln's Inn Fields, LONDON WC2A 3EE

Chartered Building Societies Institute:** 19 Baldock St, Ware, HERTS SG12 9DH

Chartered Institute of Bankers:* 11 Lombard St, LONDON EC3V 9AS

Chartered Institute of Building:* Englemere, Kings Ride, Ascot, BERKS SL5 8BJ

Chartered Institute of Loss Adjusters: 376 Strand, LONDON WC2R 0LR

Chartered Institute of Management Accountants:* 63 Portland Place, LONDON W1N 4AB

Chartered Institute of Patent Agents: Staple Inn Buildings, High Holborn, LONDON WC1V 7PZ

Chartered Institute of Publicc Finance & Accountancy: 3 Robert St, LONDON WC2N 6BH

Chemical Industries Association: Kings Buildings, Smith Square, LONDON SW1P 3JJ

The China Clay & Ball Clay Industries Training Board: John Keay House, St Austell, CORNWALL PL25 4DJ

City & Guilds of London Institute:* 76 Portland Place, LONDON W1N 4AA

The Civil Engineering Construction Conciliation Board: Federation of Civil Engineering Contractors, Cowdray House, 6 Portugal St, LONDON WC2 2HH

College of Preceptors:* Coppice Row, Theydon Bois, ESSEX CM16 7DN

College of Radiographers:* 14 Upper Wimpole St, LONDON W1M 8BN

Computing Services Industry Training Council: 16 South Molton St, LONDON W1Y 1DE

Construction Industry Training Board:** Bircham Newton Training Centre, Kings Lynn, NORFOLK PE31 6RH

Construction Industry Training Board (Northern Ireland):* 17 Cromlin Rd, Nutts Corner, DUNDROD BT29 4SR

Contract Flooring Association: Long Furlong House, Holt, NORFOLK NR25 7DD

Electricity Training Association Employee Relations Department:* 30 Millbank, LONDON SW1P 4RD

Engineering Training Authority:* PO Box 148, 41 Clarendon Rd, Watford, HERTS WD1 1HS

Engineering Training Council (Northern Ireland): First Floor, 48 Waring St, BELFAST BT1 2ED

Faculty of Teachers in Commerce: 1 The Old School, Pant Glas, OSWESTRY SY10 7HS

Federation of Civil Engineering Contractors: Cowdray House, 6 Portugal St, LONDON WC2A 2HH

Forestry Training Council: 231 Costorphine Rd, EDINBURGH EH12 7AT

Glass Training Limited:* BGMC Building, Northumberland Rd, SHEFFIELD S10 2UA

Guild of Architectural Ironmongers: 8 Stepney Green, LONDON E1 3JU

Guild of Cleaners & Launderers:** The Old Granary, Colwinston, Cowbridge, SOUTH GLAMORGAN CF7 7NJ

Guild of Professional Toastmasters: 12 Little Bornes, Alleyn Park, Dulwich, LONDON SE21 8SE

Hairdressing Training Board:** 3 Chequer Rd, DONCASTER DN1 2AA

Health and Beauty Therapy Training Board: 109 Felpham Rd, Felpham, WEST SUSSEX PO22 7PW

Heating, Ventilating & Domestic Engineers Nat. Joint Indust. Council:** ESCA House, 34 Palace Court, LONDON W2 4JG

Hotel and Catering Training Company: International House, High St, Ealing, LONDON W5 5DB

Incorporated Society of Valuers & Auctioneers: 3 Cadogan Gate, LONDON SW1X 0AS

Institute of Baths & Recreation Management:** 36–38 Sherrard St, Melton Mowbray, LEICS LE13 1XJ

Institute of Brewing:* 33 Clarges St, LONDON W1Y 8EE

Institute of Builders Merchants: Parnall House, 5 Parnall, Rd, Staple Tye, Harlow, ESSEX CN18 7PP

Institute of Carpenters: PO Box 11, Aldershot, HANTS GU11 1YW

Institute of Chartered Accountants: PO Box 433, Chartered Accountants Hall, Moorgate Place, LONDON EC2P 2BJ

Institute of Chartered Secretaries & Administrators: 16 Park Crescent, LONDON W1N 4AH

Institute of Chartered Shipbrokers: 24 St Mary Axe, LONDON EC3A 8DE

Institute of Clerk of Works of Great Britain (Inc.): 41 The Mall, LONDON W5 3TJ

Institute of Company Accountants:* 40 Tyndalls Park Rd, BRISTOL BS8 1PL

Institute of Credit Management: Easton House, Easton on the Hill, Stamford, LINCS PE9 3NH

Institute of Electrolysis Ltd: 251 Seymour Grove, MANCHESTER M16 0DS

Institute of Export: 64 Clifton St, LONDON EC2A 4HB

Institute of Financial Accountants:* 44 London Rd, Sevenoaks, KENT TN13 1AS

Institute of Health Services Management:* 75 Portland Place, LONDON W1N 4AN

Institute of Internal Auditors: 13 Abbeville Mews, 88 Clapham Park Rd, LONDON SW4 7BX

Institute of Linguists: 24A Highbury Grove, LONDON N5 2EA

Institute of Masters of Wine: Five Kings House, Kennet Wharf Lane, LONDON EC4V 3BE

Institute of Materials Management:** Crankfield Institute of Technology, Crankfield, BEDFORD

Institute of Meat: Langford, BRISTOL BS18 7DY

Institute of Metal Finishing: 48 Holloway Head, BIRMINGHAM B1 1NQ

Institute of Metals:* 1 Carlton House Terrace, LONDON SW1Y 5DB

Institute of Population Registration:** 96 Herongate Rd, LONDON E12 5EQ

Institute of Professional Investigators Ltd: 31A Wellington St, St Johns, BLACKBURN BB1 8AF

Institute of Quality Assurance:* 10 Grosvenor Gardens, LONDON SW1 0DQ

Institute of Sales Marketing Management:* 31 Upper George St, LUTON LU1 2RD

Institute of Trichologists (Inc.):* 228 Stockwell Rd, LONDON SW9 9SU

Joint Awarding Bodies:** see BTEC, C&G, CCETSW

Joint Council for the Building & Civil Engineering Industry of Northern Ireland: Federation of Building & Civil Engineering Contractors, 143 Malone Rd, BELFAST BT9 6SU

Joint Committee for Heavy Horse Training:** c/o British Horse Society, British Equestrian Centre, Stoneleigh, WARWICKSHIRE CV8 2LR

Joint Industry Board for the Electrical Contracting Industry: Kingswood House, 47–51 Sidcup Hill, Sidcup, KENT DA14 6HP

Law Society of England & Wales: Law Society Halls, 113 Chancery Lane, LONDON WC2A 1PL

London Chamber of Commerce and Industry Examinations Board:* Marlowe House, Station Rd, Sidcup, KENT DA15 7BJ

Man-Made Fibres Industry Training Advisory Board:* Central House, Gate Lane, Sutton Coldfield, WEST MIDLANDS B73 5TS

Marine and Engineering Training Association: Rycote Place, Court Rd, LONDON SE9 5N

Ministry of Defence (Army Department):** Head Army Education Eltham Place, Court Rd, LONDON SE9 5NR

National Examinations Board for Agriculture, Horticulture & Allied Industries: 46 Britannia St, LONDON WC1X 9RG

National Federation of Roofing Contractors: Education Offices, 42 Forest Green Rd, BIRMINGHAM B27 6QA

National Institute of Carpet Fitters: Wira House, West Park Ring Rd, LEEDS LS16 6QL

National Institute of Medical Herbalists Ltd: 41 Hatherley Rd, Winchester, HANTS SO22 6RR

National Joint Council for the Building Industry: 18 Mansfield St, LONDON W1M 9FG

National Joint Council for the Flat Glass Industry: 44-48 Borough High St, LONDON SE1 1YB

National Joint Council for the Flat Roofing Contracting Industry:* Fields House, Gower Rd, Haywards Heath, WEST SUSSEX RH16 4PL

National Joint Council for laying side of the Mastic Asphalt Industry: 74 Camberwell Church St, LONDON SE5 8QZ

National Joint Council for the Motor Vehicle Retail & Repair Industry:* 201 Great Portland St, LONDON W1N 6AB

National Joint Training Committee for Young Heavy Goods Vehicle Drivers: c/o RTITB, Capitol House, Empire Way, Wembley, MIDDLESEX HA9 0NG

National Pony Society: Horsehill Farm, Bagber Common, Nr Sturminster Newton, DORSET

National Proficiency Tests Council for Agriculture and Horticulture:* National Agricultural Centre, Tenth St, Stoneleigh, WARWICKSHIRE CV8 2LG

National Retail Training Council:* 4th Floor, Bedford House, 69-79 Fulham High St, LONDON SW6 3JW

National Textile Training Group, Knitting and Lace Industries Resources Agency:** 7 Gregory Boulevard, NOTTINGHAM NG7 6LD

National Wholesale Training Council:* Regency Court Business Centre, 62-66 Deansgate, MANCHESTER M3 2EN

Oil & Colour Chemists Association: 967 Harrow Rd, Wembley, MIDDLESEX HA0 2SF

Petroleum Training Federation:** Room 326, 162-168 Regent St, LONDON W1R 5TB

Pianoforte Tuners Association: 10 Reculver Rd, Herne Bay, KENT CT6 6LD

Pitman Examinations Institute:* Gatteshall Manor, Godalming, SURREY GU7 1UU

Pony Trekking & Riding Society of Wales:** Pengelli Fach Farm, Pontsticill, Vaynor nr MERTHYR TYDFIL CF48 2TU

Qualifications for Industry Ltd:* 80 Richardshaw Lane, Pudsey, LEEDS LS28 6BN

Racing and Thoroughbred Breeding Training Board:** 42 Portman Square, LONDON W1H 0EN

Rating & Valuation Association: 41 Doughty St, LONDON WC1N 2LF

Refractories, Clay Pipes & Allied Industries Training Council:* c/o University of Sheffield School of Materials, Elmfield, Northumberland Rd, SHEFFIELD S10 2TZ

Road Transport Industry Training Board:* Capitol House, Empire Way, Wembley, MIDDLESEX HA9 0NG

Road Transport Industry Training Board (Northern Ireland):* Cromlin Rd, Nutts Corner, DUNDROD BT29 4SR

Royal College of General Practitioners: 14 Princes Gate, LONDON SW7 1PU

Royal College of Pathologists: 2 Carlton House Terrace, LONDON SW1Y 5AF

Royal College of Physicians of London: 11 St Andrews Place, Regents Park, LONDON NW1 4LE

Royal College of Psychiatrists: 17 Belgrave Square, LONDON SW1X 8PG

Royal College of Surgeons of England: 35–43 Lincoln Inn Fields, LONDON WC2A 3PN

RSA Examinations Board:* Progress House, Westwood Way, COVENTRY CV4 8HS

Scottish Vocational Education Council:* Hanover House, 24 Douglas St, GLASGOW G2 7NQ

Sea Fish Industry Authority:** Industrial Development Unit, St Andrew's Dock, HULL HU3 4QE

Securities Association: The Stock Exchange, Old Broad St, LONDON EC2N 1HP

Society of Designer Craftsmen: 24 Rivington St, LONDON EC2A 3DU

Society of Dyers & Colourists:* PO Box 244, 82 Gratton Rd, BRADFORD BD1 2JB

Society of Indexers: 16 Green Rd, Birchington, KENT CT7 9JZ

Society of Investment Analysts:* 211–213 High St, BROMLEY BR1 1NY

Society of Shoe Fitters: 28 Admirals Walk, Hingham, NORWICH NR9 4JL

Steel Industry Lead Body:** Central Training Unit, Open Learning Development Unit, PO Box 32, Sheffield Rd, ROTHERHAM S60 1AG

Telecommunications Vocational Standards Council: First floor, Dacum House, Presley Way, Crownhill, MILTON KEYNES MK8 0HD

Tobacco Industry Training Organization:* Glen House, Stag Place, LONDON SW1E 5A

United Kingdom Central Council for Nursing, Midwifery and Health Visitors:* 23 Portland Place, LONDON W1N 3AF

Other addresses

Open College: St James's Building, Oxford Street, MANCHESTER M1 6FQ
Tel: 071 935 8088
Fax: 071 935 0415

Open University: Walton Hall, Milton Keynes, BUCKS MK7 6AA
Tel: 0908 274066
Fax: 0908 655898

Appendix 4

MCI Cross-referencing Form

Unit Number _____ Unit Title _____

Element of Competence Number _____											
		Performance Criteria									
		a	b	c	d	e	f	g	h	i	j
Evidence Number	Content										

Index